# The Act of Seeing

# The Act of Seeing

Essays and Conversations

# Wim Wenders

translated by Michael Hofmann

*faber and faber*
LONDON · BOSTON

First published in Germany in 1992
by Verlag der Autoren, Frankfurt, West Germany

First published in the UK in 1997
by Faber and Faber Limited
3 Queen Square London WC1N 3AU

Photoset by Parker Typesetting Service, Leicester
Printed in England by Clays Ltd, St Ives plc

A CIP record for this book
is available from the British Library
ISBN 0-571-17843-X

10 9 8 7 6 5 4 3 2 1

# CONTENTS

## PART V

## PART VI

## PART VII

In the past artists represented things they had seen on earth, things they liked seeing or might have liked to see. Today they reveal the relativity of visible things; they express their belief that the visible is only an isolated aspect in relation to the universe as a whole, and that other, invisible truths are the overriding factors. Things appear to assume a broader and more diversified meaning, often seeming to contradict the rational experience of yesterday. The artist strives to express the essential character of the accidental.

Paul Klee, Berlin 1920

(from Felix Klee, *Paul Klee* tr. Richard and Clara Winston, George Braziller Inc., 1962)

PART I

## To the End of the World
Very first treatment for a film project

Images. In the amorous realm, the most painful wounds are inflicted more often by what one sees than by what one knows.

From Roland Barthes *A Lover's Discourse*
(translated by Richard Howard, Hill & Wang, 1978)

A LOVE FILM.
A FILM ABOUT LOVE.
EVEN IF NO ONE KNOWS WHAT THAT IS.
A FILM OF DISCOVERY, THEN.

And because you can only have a film ABOUT something
if it becomes what it is about,
this film ABOUT LOVE
will be a film IN
        OF
        FOR
        WITH
        FROM
        PRO and
        CONTRA LOVE.

## *Highly Personal Preface*

It's surely no exaggeration to say that in the whole history of the cinema, no subject has been handled as much as 'love'. That's what audiences have always been interested in seeing. But it's probably also true to say that nothing nowadays is as confusing or perplexing to people as 'love'. RIEN NE VA PLUS.

That's how it seems. Wherever you look. And for a long time now, people have given up hope of getting any guidance or understanding of 'love' from the cinema. The cinema has messed up its biggest subject, basically spreading mis- or dis-information about 'love'. Or is it that 'love', and cinema, and pictures, just didn't go together?

Certainly, books are more to the point. Because there the reader's imagination is in play.

A long way away, in Sydney, someone asked me after a screening of *Paris, Texas*: 'Is that a true story?' I said: 'It is now.'

And suddenly I was more convinced than ever that in films, with and through images, a kind of storytelling was once again possible, even necessary, that would resolve the paradox of 'true stories'.

At that moment I felt a kind of boundless confidence in cinema, which is still with me, and so I know that, come what may, I now have to tell that story that up until now I've been running away from: a love story. Have to.

A story in which love is possible, love works, is right and proper, and with an ending to match. At any price. All received wisdom to the contrary. (And where did that ever get us.) With a courage born of despair. With fortune favouring the brave. In spite of everything and, if need be, TO THE END OF THE WORLD.

## The Story Itself

is very simple. Maybe it'll become more complicated. We'll see. At any rate I'd like to make this film in the same way I made *Alice in the Cities*, *Kings of the Road*, *The State of Things*, and, not least, the second half of *Paris, Texas*.

Use an almost empty 'narrative structure' and gradually have it filled in by the actors and by pooling all our experience. Discover the story, in other words.

It's the only way I can do it now. And there's no better way of making an adventure film.

The backbone will be provided by an itinerary which I myself will have followed at least once in its entirety before shooting begins. Most of the places on it I know well. After the journey there will be a long and tight narrative, though still not in dialogue form, on the basis of which the production team will be able to come up with some fairly precise budget estimates, and which will make the scale of the adventure clear to the actors and all those involved.

A screenplay writer willing to take on the story and its parameters will be recruited.

## The Story Again

in brief.

A woman, in love with a man who – for good reason, he believes – is running away from her, pursues him round the world. She in turn is pursued by another man who is in love with *her*, but whom she is no longer in love with. All three are pursued by a couple of crooks who want their money back. (They stole it from a bank, and the woman stole it from them, in order to be able to pursue her beloved.) And then there's a detective, who is engaged first by the woman, and then in succession by all the other parties, to follow whoever it happens to be, or, alternatively, to try and shake them off. So it's not all that simple after all, especially when everything takes place in the course of a pretty breathtaking journey. In the end, our detective doesn't have an employer, but will still be hot on the trail, because by then he will be head over heels in love with the woman himself. And at the very end it will transpire that in all this stop-go loving, there will only have been one real love.

## One thing is clear,

even in this brief account:
for all the emotional drama, there will be times in this story in which our heroes won't take themselves entirely seriously. And that, as I understand it, is the only real premise for COMEDY.

## The Itinerary

begins in Venice, leads across the South of France to Paris, and from there to Frankfurt and Berlin, and then, by way of Lisbon and London, will leave Europe altogether and head for Tokyo. Then from Tokyo, via a South Sea island, to San Francisco, and via Cuba to Rio de Janeiro and then across to Dakar. From there through the Sahara to Casablanca, and finally by ship to the place where the story originally began, Venice.

Not all the characters will make it to the end alive. A few will 'fall by the wayside'.

*May 1984.*

## Travelling in time
From the conversation with Wolfram Schütte about his new film,
the European cinema and Germany

WOLFRAM SCHÜTTE: *Our meeting is taking place at the Rhine-Main
Airport. You've arrived from Düsseldorf, and are on your way to Venice,
two days later you'll be back in Berlin. Still engaged on your 'work in
progress'. A new film whose preparations, worldwide, have kept you busy
these past several years. How is the work progressing –* To the End of the
World?

WIM WENDERS: Two months ago we finally got the financial backing
sorted out. It just seemed to take forever. If you remember, I was even
working on it for a couple of years before *Wings of Desire*. But now
everything's set: the backing, the script, cast and shooting schedule. The
filming will begin on 2 April.

*Who wrote the screenplay?*

I wrote it together with the Australian author Peter Carey, based on a
story I'd developed over the last several years with Solveig (Dommartin).
Carey is my sort of age, and he's a well-known writer in the English-
speaking world.

*How did you happen to choose him?*

When I began work on the screenplay five years ago, I happened to come
across a volume of his short stories. It was called *The Fat Man in History*.
It was his first book, and I thought they were fantastic stories. I read them
in Australia, and because the film is half set in Australia, I was looking for
someone who could offer an Australian angle. I asked him if he might be
interested, but he turned me down, he'd just embarked on a novel. So
Solveig and I went on working on the screenplay by ourselves for a while,
and then with help from an American writer. We got one draft finished,
then I didn't have any money, and we had to switch to another project.

After *Wings of Desire* I said to myself we should make a completely fresh start. Then I tried Peter Carey again, his novel had come out by now, and he had some time, and so we spent the last couple of years, with interruptions, working on six different drafts; the last of them I'm very satisfied with, and we're rehearsing it now.

*How long is the film going to be – all your recent work (and some of your earlier films too) has been on the long side?*

The contract specifies 2 hours and 45 minutes. It mustn't be any longer than that. And of course the distributor would prefer it to be a bit shorter.

*What countries will you be filming in, I think I heard someone say there were going to be seventeen?*

Well, we've got it down to twelve, otherwise it couldn't have been affordable: in Europe, Asia, America, Australia and Africa. We have a 20 million dollar budget. It's one long story, with elements of love and chase and sci-fi in it, set between 1999 and 2001. The shooting schedule will follow the itinerary . . .

*. . . the way you shot* Kings of the Road, *following the East German border . . .*

. . . across five continents. We're travelling with a really compact team of just twenty-two people, and in every country we film in we'll take on extra crew for lights, production and props, so that the total number of people involved will be in the hundreds. All the film will be sent back to Germany, where it will be immediately developed, and my editor Peter Przygodda, who I've been working with for twenty years now and who I trust blindly, will make a rough cut and keep me posted on the quality of the takes.

*Has your experience of German labs really been that good?*

Yes, in this case Arri will be doing it, because we'll be working with a new prototype of an Arri 65 mm camera. Also, it will be the first film in Europe for twenty years to be shot in 70 mm.

*Who have you got playing the leads?*

The lovers will be played by Solveig Dommartin and William Hurt; other main parts by Sam Neill, an Australian actor, then Jeanne Moreau and Max von Sydow (playing the parents of the William Hurt character), and Rüdiger Vogler plays a detective. It's a German-French-Australian co-production, and a Japanese investor is coming in as well. The executive producer is an American I've known for ten years, Jonathan Taplin's his name, and among other things he's made are (Scorsese's) *Mean Streets* and *The Last Waltz*.

*In the course of this extensive pre-production you've got around a lot, in Europe and elsewhere. How would you judge the future in film-political terms here?*

The European cinema will only be able to survive on a multinational, European basis. For some time now that's how it's been on the level of production. But it's distribution that will really determine the future of the European film. That's the $64,000 question right now. Already, it's become very very hard to get distributors to programme European films that even three or four years ago, let alone ten, would have simply automatically made it onto the screens.

*Is that true for all of Europe?*

Yes, all of it – even in France.

*Are you saying the difficulties for the European films in Europe are really just down to a 'technical' problem, like distribution? Isn't it also that the attitude of the cinema public has changed?*

Well, of course there's the phenomenon of the blockbuster. If you don't rock up with widescreen and Dolby stereo, you're going to have a hard time of it. So you have to offer cinema comfort and big screens and Dolby stereo to challenge all the advances that have been made in the other media.

*What is the impact of that on someone who's making films now in Germany? Is there still a future for the 'small feature', with lower budget, fewer star names, unsensational subject-matter and so on?*

I don't think you can see that in isolation. For the 'small feature' to continue to exist in Europe, you also need the big 'spectacular' to hold the door open for it, if you like. If the gulf between the little 'art-house movie' and the trashy monster film goes on widening, and there's nothing at all in the middle, then pretty soon we will wake up and find the little films are all gone. For me, *Paris, Texas* and *Wings of Desire* weren't just successful films in their own right, they also helped keep the door open for the kind of cinema they represent. I'm looking to do that in *To the End of the World* as well, albeit on a bigger scale. As I say, it's the first European film since the 1960s to be shot in 70 mm and if you look at who's appearing in it and so on, it's a 'big film' by anyone's definition; but at the same time, it'll still be an *auteur* film, a Wim Wenders film. I hope it'll help keep our screens open for things that aren't *Rambo* and that aren't American.

*Fine, but* Paris, Texas *came out in 1984, it's 1990 now, so in six years you've made just two big films: what sort of impact is that going to make against the monster imports?*

I'm sure the coarsening of the public's sensibilities has gone on apace; films are becoming increasingly 'invisible', if you like. Things like irony or ambivalence are getting harder and harder to pick up. That's to do with media saturation, the audience is being deluged with so much stuff, and with the fact that so much of what we see and hear nowadays is turned right up. Anything with nuances in it is simply washed away.

*But isn't one of the points of 'postmodernism' supposed to be that a mosaic of different experiences and sensations builds up a more differentiated perception . . .?*

But it's so absurd, because something first needs to be presented to the public as 'worth experiencing' – for instance a 'little film' turns up that's suddenly hailed as 'an event'. That promotes it right away into a different category, and suddenly everyone's eager to go and see it. So whatever isn't a 'media event' doesn't count. There aren't enough people who are prepared to discover things for themselves. Everybody knows that there is such a thing as the 'little film', but they're only prepared to give one a chance if it's been pronounced great. That even happens now in France, where previously loads of little films could get by on audiences of 20 to 100,000 in Paris. That used to be quite a broad field, and the films made their money back just on the box office. But even in Paris nowadays a 'little film' only makes it by becoming some kind of event. It's all become terribly American: you don't get anywhere unless the media get their teeth into it. That means that advertising and promotion become part of the production budget – the big American films spend more on that than on the production itself. And that's the trend now, even with 'little films'.

*What role do you see for film reviewing in all this?*

The kind of thing you practise and I appreciate – that type of reviewing has become almost irrelevant. It's only used as a source of quotes. People just want to read the quotes, and that makes the reviewer into a kind of unpaid promoter.

*Which corresponds to the status of cinema itself as a glorified launchpad for TV and video.*

That's right. I see more and more instances of films being launched with a great fanfare, and then silence, because the only point of the fanfare was to get the video sales going. All the hoopla about the film was only created to sell cassettes or publicize transmission on pay-TV or something. 'Canal Plus' in France shows films concurrently with the cinema première – and obviously for the producer that ends up being more important than the trouble and unpredictability of a first run in a cinema.

*Are exploitation practices very different in the different European countries?*

They are. The English are way ahead, the Germans thank God are still quite backward because the privatization of TV started here so much later. But it's on its way now. We've already felt some of the effects. The German video rights to *Paris, Texas* and *Wings of Desire* hadn't been sold, but you could already buy the tapes: they were imported from England; it was especially upsetting with *Paris, Texas*, because the film was in English anyway; it didn't matter so much with *Desire*: who here wants to watch a German film with English subtitles?

*You're shooting a film in 70 mm, I take it there are enough cinemas here that are suitably equipped to show it?*

Yes, there are seven in Berlin alone, and around about eighty in the Federal Republic. Whether they're all as well equipped as one might wish is open to question. But maybe they'll pull their socks up, because it's a great thing to be able to say, 'Here in the original 70 mm version' – that pulls in the crowds. Arriflex have invested huge sums in developing the camera we're going to use to make our film. They see it as an investment for the 1990s, and it looks as though in future more films will be made in that format, to be able to offer a much better picture in competition with TV.

*And what do your backers in TV have to say to that?*

They show a scaled-down copy of the film anyway. It doesn't matter that much. TV's a bit less afraid than it used to be of the black borders at the top and bottom of the screen. Their market research people have told them that the viewers see the black borders as a token of quality. Especially the younger ones: if there's a black bit at the top, that means it's a 'film', and so it's bound to be good. I've seen it happen with kids myself. Black bits equals cinema. They'd rather watch that than most other types of programmes.

*Do you have much contact with younger German directors?*

Last year I saw a lot of impressive first films, and I know a few of the younger people very well; but I don't yet feel old enough to want to see myself as any kind of 'father figure' to them. They have a much harder time of it than we ever did. We were really quite lucky when we started out. By now, it's a real fight to get to make your first film. And the first one's not even the hardest, most of them manage that pretty well. It's the second one that is really hell, that's the real test case. And if you succeed with your second, your third is actually where you embark on a career as a film-maker and try and establish some sense of identity in the film landscape: all that takes so much more strength than it cost us. It was so much easier, TV was more prepared to take a chance, and so were public funding bodies; audiences used to be more receptive, even though we used to complain that we didn't have a ready-made audience waiting for us, but still there was a *potential* audience. Today you have trouble finding even a potential audience for an ambitious or a difficult film.

Sometimes I get the feeling I'm in the way; I've helped out the odd director making his or her first or second feature, though I told myself it's not necessarily the right thing to do, it might saddle them with being thought of as my protégés. All I really did for Jim Jarmusch was give him some stock, and that was a kind of albatross he carried around with him for years.

Through my work for the society that provides the support for the European Film Prize, I have more contact with European directors. It's quite striking at the moment how much more solidarity there is on all kinds of European levels than there is on the national scene, where it's often a case of dog eat dog; it's so competitive. I don't presently see a way into the European level for the younger people. All those European institutions are just after famous names and faces to grace their letterheads. Along with a few other people, I'm trying to make it possible for the next generation to get in there. You've no idea how hard it is.

*Can we talk about what everybody's talking about right now. Where were you when they opened the Berlin Wall?*

I was in Australia, in the middle of the desert.

*Since when, what time did you get there?*

I left when people were still being put on trains to get them out of the German embassies, end of September time, and it wasn't till mid-December that I got back to Berlin. So I missed out on everything that happened in between. I was in the middle of the Australian desert, miles away from any telephone, and I caught the opening of the Wall three days late. My office in Berlin was faxing me bits of newspapers. I kept trying to ring them, and finally the office started sending me photographs so I could see the incredible scenes for myself. My only concern was always, because things reached me so late, that it might all already be over, and the Russian tanks might have rolled in.

*How did you find it when you did finally get back?*

Everything was different. I couldn't even get home, it was all jam-packed. I live in Kreuzberg, and the views from my flat are more of East Berlin than West, and the street itself is quiet except when there are demos; but

now it was stuffed full of Skodas and Ladas and Trabbis. And the din! I
live next to the Wall, and sleep with my windows open, and they were
hammering away like woodpeckers, even at night, it was amazing . . . I
only took part in one actual celebration, at New Year; I was in East Berlin
for that.

*What does 'Germany' mean to you, or Berlin?*

When I came back from America – after my experiences in Hollywood – I
had my strongest and clearest sense of 'Germany' in East Berlin. I could
feel it in the pit of my stomach, which never happened in West Berlin, or
here in Frankfurt. If I go into the city [Frankfurt] from here, it's really no
different than London, Sydney or Paris. East Berlin, on the other hand, is
like travelling back into my childhood: back to Germany. The Russian
influence there is much less significant than the American and the general
Western way of life is over here.

*How about a phenomenological impression? Squares, streets, buildings,
faces?*

I think most of all of people's faces and gestures and clothing. That's the
Germany of my earliest childhood memories, or from the German cinema
of the 1920s. That doesn't exist here any more. But in East Berlin I saw:
this is where it all came from, this is 'Germany'.

*Don't you think you're being nostalgic?*

Not really nostalgic, that would mean missing it and longing for it. But I
was deeply *moved* by seeing and feeling that 'Germany', because it isn't
me any more, I'm a cosmopolite now.

But at the same time: through the German language, through my
parents, my early years – that all gave me a sense of home, and nothing
has ever evoked that for me so strongly as East Berlin. To get on a tram or
ride the U-Bahn in East Berlin: for me that's like a trip into Germany. They
have a different way of dealing with each other, and there I suddenly get a
sense of my own Germanness.

*Your 'German-ness'? What does that really mean to you? I suppose in
France you would be thought of as a German director . . .*

I'm not so sure. Certainly the Americans see me as a German director. As for myself, finally and irrevocably, I'm a *European* director; but, just as irrevocably, through my childhood and my earliest memories, I'm German. And somewhere out of all that is where the films come from. You have some sort of a nest in your head that contains a fixed number of stories, no more and no fewer. They come from childhood and from dreams, there's no getting around it: you can't invent anything that wasn't already somewhere inside you to begin with.

*Following* Paris, Texas *you did, in some sense, and to some people's surprise, 'return' in* Wings of Desire. *But now, with* To the End of the World, *you're leaving us again . . .*

I wouldn't put it like that, and not just because a fair bit of the new film is set in Berlin too. I'm not 'leaving' – because the film shows that the whole world has become just *one* place. The assumption I'm making is that 'for the whole world' travelling has become much more taken for granted even than it was just ten years ago; and in another ten years, the time the film is set, maybe Frankfurt Airport will just seem like an underground station.

*Recent events in Eastern Europe and the GDR must have thrown out your plans for* To the End of the World . . .?

Well, Moscow and Berlin are two of the cities we're filming in, and so of course we had to do quite a bit of rewriting. The screenplay version I took along with me to Australia had the Wall coming down in 1999, and there were a whole lot of scenes showing that event. Of course, when I came back, all that was impossible. So we rewrote it, and the Moscow episode too looks very different to our original draft of a couple of years ago.

*How is it for you, now you've come back from Australia to a different country – what kind of 'Germany' is it you see now?*

Let me answer that in a roundabout sort of way. Last year I travelled a ridiculous amount, I've never travelled like that, sometimes I'd be on three continents in the space of a week. The craziest journey of all saw me in Moscow and Tokyo on the same day.

And that was also the *longest* journey I've made in my life: because it covered about thirty years. Not just in terms of lifestyle or technological development, but thirty years of learning or understanding. When I was in Tokyo and I thought of my phantom film-makers in Moscow, rediscovering the American underground movies of the 1960s, it made me sad because I thought: How would they get on in Tokyo? Because either they've already reached the year 2000 in Tokyo, or else the people in Moscow are still hopelessly stuck in the 1960s or 70s.

In other words: my travels over the past year were as much time-travel as just changing places. In Australia, for instance, I met people, even got to be friends with some of them, who are the first generation to meet the 'white man', so effectively they grew up in the Stone Age. In that way the time-travelling within Australia was the strangest thing of all.

That's what leads me to think that what needs to happen in Germany is a time problem: two different time-periods need to be brought together. You can't do that just by turning them into a *single* German state. That would be catastrophic. It's a bandwagon that a lot of politicians are jumping on to, and it terrifies me. The CDU were in trouble, now those 'Helmut, Helmut' chants have given them a terrific boost. For the politicians to call for German unity without giving a thought to the winners and losers is just absurd, because the people aren't ready for it, living in their two distinct time-zones. I don't know what you can do about that; all I think is this: that it will take a lot of time and a great deal of travelling in time to get it accomplished.

That nationalist, Greater German tone that you get on this side is horrible to me, shockingly conceited. All that condescension about taking in 'poor relations' makes a mockery of a historical situation in which we were simply the lucky ones. That's really not the way to do it.

*The time-travelling in your life, I take it, is largely to do with the preparations for your new film?*

The story of the film (which we're setting in 1999) has a bit to do with the way our current time-travelling will be planed down. In my version of it, Moscow will then be a more interesting place to be than San Francisco. The utopian aspect of the thing is that the transition to the year 2000 will happen everywhere simultaneously. That makes it a hopelessly optimistic film. What can be done about the present chronological unevennesses you experience, with the depressions you're subject to as a time-traveller?

Unless you present the gulfs as 'bridgeable'. That's the only possible way I can produce something utopian and optimistic today.

*Utopian* and *optimistic; you're not a man for dystopias are you? Why not?*

I love to look at positive utopias; even if they are sometimes terribly naive and sometimes just a bit woozy; I still find it more fruitful than dystopias. I have no interest in gloomy views of the future. The end of the world is such common currency nowadays, you can't do anything with it. All that 'no future' talk bores me to tears.

*But now, with the help of Mikhail Gorbachev, the world has changed greatly in the past four years. A lot of things have been opened up, there is less control, more freedom, more debate on a whole range of things . . .*

I agree. Thinking has opened up. But just because it's opened up – even if it's not gotten any more transparent – I think a positive utopia is a so much bolder thing than a dystopia. It's always easier – for journalism certainly, but for all other writing too – to paint a catastrophe or to create a big drama than do the opposite. 'Bad news' sells better; and so a comedy is the hardest thing to get off the ground. Maybe that's why I'm trying for a positive utopia, because I think that might be the next step on the way – who knows – to seeing the world as a comedy.

*Well now, you yourself, my dear Herr Wenders, with your grave and thoughtful manner, hardly strike me as a humorist always able to look on the bright side.*

Of course you're right; but that's also the way all humorists are, and I have a secret hope that I might one day still become one.

*First publication*: Frankfurter Rundschau, *27 January 1990*

## The Act of Seeing

It is my conviction that a film has to be preceded by a dream, either a real dream of the sort that you wake up and remember, or a daydream.

I don't want to absolutely insist on this, it probably doesn't apply to all films. A lot of films don't have any truck with dreams, they are the product of calculation, and the type of investment they represent is not emotional but financial. But I'm not concerned with them here. I'm thinking of films that have a soul, a discernible core, that radiate their own identity. These have all been 'dreamed up', of that I feel certain.

Now making a film can be a lengthy enterprise, in the course of which difficulties may arise that provoke doubts or that even cloud the original intention altogether. In such an event, you need a source of energy that won't dry up or run out. This strength, which can nourish a film from the moment of its original conception to its finished print is, for want of a better word, the 'soul' of a film, its own dream of itself. (Which isn't to say that a film has to end up looking just like its own first dream-image; on the contrary, the strength of its 'dream' is what will permit the film to survive intact all its bruising encounters with reality and whatever new conditions are imposed on it, and keep it open to all manner of change, departure and topsy-turviness.)

What was the dream behind *To the End of the World*, what kept it going these past twelve years? What was its 'ur-image'? The love story, the science fiction film, the road movie? Or a combination of all three? It seems to me that from the outset there was something else behind it which had the strength to hold together these disparate elements, a theme they all held in common.

I remember in my first notebook for the film noting something from Roland Barthes's *A Lover's Discourse*: 'Images. In the amorous realm, the most painful wounds are inflicted more often by what one sees than by what one knows.' Mysterious though that sentence seemed to me at first, I felt right away how relevant it was to our film – nothing more than a plan at the time – because of the way it brought together the three ideas of 'love', 'images' and 'seeing'.

But how can 'images' or 'seeing' be the subject for a film, for a love story even? Isn't there something redundant in the idea of a 'film about seeing'? Or could a science fiction film perhaps shed some new light on it?

The desire to make a science fiction film is largely motivated by the extraordinary imaginative freedom the form gives you. You can really do pretty much anything in it. The further into the future you go, the more freedom you have. (The thing that often bothers me about science fiction films is when they fail to take sufficient liberties. The characters in 1950s sf films talk and act like people in the 50s did, and a thousand years from now the characters in 1970s science fiction will still come on like 70s people, they'll be there for all time, acting out their petty conflicts the way we did in our hung-up twentieth century . . .)

On the whole, it seems to me, the genre reflects the epoch from which the future is viewed much more than any real or imaginary future. I didn't suppose it would be any different with my own. Mine is a film made in 1990, and it's projected into the year 2000, so it's about my or our hopes and fears and desires today, projected into the near future. You may say not much changes in ten years. But even so: that little interval gives us the freedom to use our imagination a little, and to dream up things that, to date, don't exist.

What was it that most interested me about the future? Would people behave differently towards one another? Looking back over the 1970s and 80s, it seemed to me you could observe small changes in behaviour, in people's attitudes and interactions. So we tried to build some of that into the screenplay and the acting; we made some encounters more direct and immediate, brusquer than they probably would be today. Even so, it did seem far-fetched to want to show a love story happening in a completely different way than it would now, or that men and women would somehow behave with each other in some radically different way. In any case, our story was already the reversal of one of the oldest stories about men and women: in *Peer Gynt*, Solveig spends a lifetime waiting for her husband to return to her as he promised to do, which he finally does once he's been all over the world. In our version Solveig (sic) doesn't wait for one second, she takes off after him. Or, to put it another way, using the oldest version of that story: Penelope doesn't stay at home, she follows Odysseus and tries to catch him up. There was the connection between the love story and the road movie.

Travel, or people's attitude towards travel, would certainly continue to change in the future. Looking back, it seemed to me that it was precisely here that huge advances have been made in the last couple of decades. People travel more and more, more and more 'naturally', go for longer and longer distances. The aeroplane, once a privileged means of transport, has become quite ordinary. It seems the earth really is shrinking. In a further ten years, people will doubtless have made still more progress, and be on the move still more.

Looking back on it, though, what has changed most between the 1960s and 70s and now is the way people are used to dealing with images. It was completely inconceivable not so long ago – the mass of images we deal with – inconceivable twenty years ago, all those tiny portable video gadgets like the Handycam and Watchman and what all, which children these days know how to use; completely inconceivable too the easy access to all manner of images. Plus, an ever more confident use of computers, and the world of images associated with that, video games, etc., etc. The next phase, 'virtual reality', is very close, and the step to digitalized image-banks is imminent too. Even High Definition is already a reality, though not yet universally accessible.

So the most alluring thing to me was to use a science fiction film to think about how we might deal with images in the future, and to use that imaginative freedom to reflect on 'the future of seeing'. Is there such a thing? Is seeing even something that could change?

The most utopian aspect of all this seemed to me the possibility that blind people might one day be able to see. Even as a child, I used to think about blindness a lot. It was to do with one of my childhood fantasies – a scientist who was able to show images to blind people. That hero of my childhood became Dr Heinrich Farber, whose dream it is to have his blind wife Edith see again. And that was the connection between a love story and the subject of 'seeing', and in two variations too: the love story of a couple nearing the end of their lives, carrying on into the story of a young couple. Sam, going around collecting images for his mother on behalf of his father, meets Claire, who falls in love with him. Those three seemingly disparate strands were now tightly interwoven.

Of course we didn't want to have some childishly utopian version of how Dr Farber could show his blind wife images. After a lot of research and conversations with eye specialists and also with computer people and biochemists, we came up with – this was all in the preparation phase of the film – a document we called *The Act of Seeing*, which I'd simply like to quote for you here.

How might a blind person learn to see in the future? At the moment, and for some time to come, eye transplants appear impossible. Not a realistic prospect. To connect the optic nerve in a new eye with the visual centre in the brain will still be a dream in the year 2000, just as now. Therefore we will have to think of ways of bypassing the eyes. How might that be done? Electronically perhaps?

By the year 2000 there will be computers with the ability to 'see'. Years of programming with ever more detailed information will enable them to distinguish between different colours, shapes and outlines, and to read them. Computers will be able to scan and interpret images. They will be able to 'look at' an image and to 'recognize' what it's of. They will be able to distinguish between images, between a dog and a cat, a man and a woman, one face from another face. That is the first part of the idea.

The other part of the idea: to have a sighted person see on behalf of a blind one. A 'cameraman' will look through a camera, which he will wear like a helmet or special goggles, and the camera will take High Definition video recordings of exactly what he sees. Simultaneous recordings of the sound will be made by Kunstkopf. The result is an 'objective document' of what the cameraman has seen. Now that isn't even utopian, it's already possible in principle. But it doesn't help the blind person. It's not enough just to come up with the 'objective image'. On the same bit of tape, then, an extra bit of data will be recorded, some parallel information: the brain activity of the cameraman doing the recording. A huge number of electrodes to register in highest possible resolution the electromagnetic impulses in the visual centre of the seeing person, to record, so to speak, the *Act of Seeing* itself. That information, though it might be cacophonous and amorphous to begin with, is the 'subjective image'. The more precision, concentration and emotional involvement the cameraman or camerawoman brings to the 'objective image', the more complex and many-layered and accurate the 'subjective image' will become. This recording process is referred to as 'first sight'.

Both sets of data from the 'first sight' process are stored on one tape and fed into an enormous computer, which mixes the electromagnetic impulses of the brain and the actual image. Because the computer can recognize images, it 'understands' the 'objective image'. The 'subjective image', though, remains bewildering to the computer. In order to be able to decipher the innumerable impulses from the brain plasma, in other words in order to understand which impulses relate to which parts of the image, how what has been seen is converted into brain data, for those things the computer needs an extra key, an additional source of knowledge that will permit it to make a selection and crack the code.

The cameraman who made the first recording undergoes a process that for the sake of simplicity we've called 'second sight'. In a darkened, sound-proofed room, he is confronted with the images he has recorded himself. A High Definition monitor replays him his own recordings. This time too the computer records his brain activity. Because he already knows the images, this is an act of re-seeing, of recognition, of memory. The computer tracks his eye-movements over the screen, and while recording his 'second sight', since it's also programmed with the objective and subjective images of his 'first sight', it can finally get to work: from all the raw information, it can filter out which brain signals correspond to which images. This layering of different data works as a sort of sieve, and the computer is now in a position to build up a new 'subjective image' from the sifted data made up entirely from brain signals. The resulting patterns are relayed to the blind person's optic centre, on the assumption that a visual experience will be triggered there that will approximate to 'seeing', and in the hope that what was recorded in the 'first sight' will be made accessible to the blind person.

The harder the sighted person concentrates while registering the images during the first and second sight, the greater the chance that the computer will be able to capture images that can be replicated in the brain of the blind person. Assisting the picture, of course, is the original sound of the recording, which is played synchronously to the blind person.

A screen would make it possible for the computer to show which image it is currently 'beaming out'. That simulation, of course, wouldn't be identical with what the blind person is seeing. One would never quite know that, and would have to rely on confirmation from the blind person.

As we worked on our screenplay, that was how we imagined Dr Heinrich Farber, with help from his son Sam, showing his wife Edith what was denied her all her life: images of her children and grandchildren, her friends, and the places in the world that have formed her life.

We thought to ourselves: 'This invention is a good and useful thing, even if still utopian.' But, as with so many 'good inventions', isn't there also the danger of some possible misuse here too? Couldn't this procedure be used in another way; in other words, mightn't the Farbers' fictional situation become the cornerstone for some possibly destructive use of the idea? If a computer is able to translate images into brain signals, then surely it could be made to do the opposite, and make images out of brain signals. And if that's possible, what's to keep it from making dreams and memories visible? Imagine seeing your dreams on a monitor, as though they were some new kind of video?

That became the last chapter of our film. And our interpretation of this future prospect of seeing was this: to look at these deepest images in the human soul can only be destructive, profoundly immoral or narcissistic. The only people in our story who are dead against it are the aborigines, who make a religion of their sacred inner images, their 'dream pictures', giving them more importance than the profane images of 'reality'. And there, in the midst of this 40,000-year-old people, twelve years ago is also where my idea of Dr Farber and his invention first came to me, as a daydream.

*First appearance: Press booklet (German language version) to accompany the release of* To the End of the World, *September 1991*

PART II

# Perceiving movement
## Conversation with Taja Gut

WIM WENDERS: You came by train: don't you like flying?

TAJA GUT: *No,\* only if I absolutely have to. A couple of years ago I had to fly to Lenigrad.*

On a Russian plane? Well, that can be pretty hairy. The whole contraption rattles and shakes like an old Beetle. Recently I flew to Moscow, and they put me in a row of seats that faced the wrong way. On the whole aeroplane there was just this one row of seats facing back, like you get on trains. Flying's bad enough already, but taking off while facing back and looking down at all the other passengers – that's hard! And then the opposite for landing, as if everyone was about to fall on top of me! I wouldn't recommend it to you.

*Your early film reviews, it seems to me, read almost like prophetic accounts of your films even before you started making them – not their subjects, but the way you treat an image. Just as surprising, so soon after 1968 and so on, was the complete absence of any political discourse, how you just talked about sensitivity and alertness and devotion, which is such a feature in your films. Where do you draw the strength to be like that, or to become like that in times like ours?*

I've no doubt I've been deeply affected by these times, but the question is how – especially in the context of '68, where I actually found myself slap bang in the middle of things, including political activism. I was living in communes, some of the people got into the terrorist scene shortly afterwards – that was the point where I quit. I suppose I always thought a lot of their ideas were really good, but their need to put them into action amounted to a kind of masochism: they were doing violence to themselves

\*This, happily, is no longer the case (Interv.).

and their feelings, so these ideas ended up destroying them, because they had nothing to do with their feelings. I have to say, I came out of that period in a very troubled state myself.

I ended up by feeling I had to start all over again, so to speak, and the only things that had any value were personal things. I felt that only private experience could be the basis for anything I had to say, that it would somehow transcend the private and acquire general validity. It was the opposite of what the '68ers believed, that they could speak in universals – the whole time they claimed they could speak on behalf of everyone – but I thought they were doing violence to themselves and to people in general.

And so I started making films that were almost confessional, like a diary. My reviews too – that was really when I went to school, writing pieces for *Filmkritik*, and then for the *Süddeutsche* and for *Die Zeit* – they were just about how I got on with films, they didn't even attempt to give a 'judgement' or say anything objective at all. And I think that that method and that attitude – that I could only talk from experience – was simply carried forward into my films.

Of course, you also keep a lot of what formed you as a child, and I think I was profoundly formed by growing up in a Catholic family, and by my father's profession. He's a surgeon, a really committed doctor, only ever concerned to help the people who came to him. It's not possible to shake off something like that, that kind of an example.

*Did you always know you wanted to make films?*

Not at all. Quite the opposite, in fact. I'd already made films, three of them, when I stopped in the middle of making the fourth and thought, hm, perhaps this isn't really an accident after all, this is actually a *way* and it could be something like a job – that was during *Alice in the Cities*. Up until then I always thought it was a great stroke of luck, a sort of freakish coincidence that I was allowed to make a film, and then a second and a third. The third was the biggest botch-up of all, it was *The Scarlet Letter*; and after it I thought, well, that's the end of that; this proves that it didn't really amount to anything. And it was only when I decided to put myself on the line, and make a film strictly according to my own principles, *Alice in the Cities*, that I suddenly realized I do have something to say in this language of film. But I was completely prepared either to go back to writing, or else take up painting again.

*You painted as well?*

I always wanted to be a painter. Before I went to film school in Munich, I studied various subjects in a half-hearted sort of way, but while I was supposed to be studying medicine and philosophy, what I was actually doing with my time was painting. So I drew my conclusions, and decided to take painting seriously. I went to Paris, and there – it was just by chance really, because it was bitterly cold all the time, and I was sitting around in an unheated flat, and the cheapest way of being in the warm was going to the *Cinémathèque*, which cost just one franc – I started to watch films. It turned into a fevered passion. I often saw as many as five or six films in a day, and in the course of a year I saw pretty much the whole repertoire. It was a kind of quick course in film history. And because there were too many films, I began to write them up for my own benefit; it seemed wrong to me that as I was watching my last film at midnight or so, I already couldn't remember what I'd seen that afternoon. That was how I first began as a film critic.

*Rock music plays a big part in all your films. You've gone out of your way to say – the same thing happened to me too – that that music saved your life.*

Sure, rock'n'roll rescued a whole generation from loneliness, and not just that, it helped it to realize its own creative potential. That was the really great thing about 60s rock'n'roll, especially the British groups: its kick, the relish it gave you for the possibilities of your own imagination. That British rock music I grew up on, second-generation rock music really – I never had a proper rapport with their predecessors, Elvis, Chuck Berry and so forth – they were people like art students and so on, who would have been stuck without it, just like me. And by starting to make music with so much vibrancy and electricity, that was what finally – I was still at school then – got me to the point of wanting to determine my own life by myself.

*Yes, it was just like that for me as well. Later, it all got a bit dubious. The originality and delight that that music conveyed later seemed rather calculated and commercially driven.*

Yes, I suppose it was bound to happen. But I don't think that's really what mattered. It was more something that came along in the 70s when it got to be openly commercial, and as someone who listened to it, you began to feel really used and bossed around. But that was really only later, the impression that your need for that music was being turned into a huge business operation. In the beginning it wasn't like that. I've always felt that right through the 60s, that music had great strength, and that it transcended any manipulation and doubt, and that rock'n'roll always kept at least the potential for that strength and that kick and that ability to rescue people. Even if it's turned into a huge global industry by now, you still occasionally encounter that strength. You just have to be a bit more discriminating when you look for it than you used to.

*Tell me something about the relationship between your films and your life. Are the films – of course they are other things too – a coming to terms with things in your life, or more a sort of projection or blueprint?*

I think the films were really always both things, that they used my past experience, and that they looked ahead into the future; each one was like throwing a stone, and I had to try and work out where it landed. But at the same time, they were all imbued with their own respective time as well. Of course, I haven't always processed my own experience; I've also used a lot of things that friends have told me or that I've observed. And from the moment I sensed that I was onto something, here's something I can work with, develop a story from – this was during *Alice in the Cities* – from that moment on I always allowed the films to improvise their own subjects during the shooting.

In other words, making films for me was being set a problem by the film, and solving it. A film was a way of getting clarification about something, learning or grasping something; sometimes it might be a rejection of something, like in *The State of Things*. Each film was always a sort of programme for the shoot, and a problem I was trying to shed light on. The couple of occasions I tried to make a film I knew in advance, it went badly wrong. *The Scarlet Letter* and *Hammett*; those films that were like an industrial product all mapped out on the drawing board – they misfired.

*Has dealing with film as a medium ever caused you problems? The illusionism of it – there isn't really any movement, just a lot of single shots – that incredible fragmentation of the process, those innumerable individual shots, generally taken and retaken, through the editing process to the end. The fragmentation for the actor too, who can only play a scene at a time. And, on the other hand, the dangers of manipulation – the ease of cutting things out of films; the financial pressures; the extremely artificial nature of the material, the violence that a film can do to habits of seeing –*

Oh yes, sure. Of course a film can exert violence or compulsion, and at any stage of its creation. Let's begin at the end: when the film is ready, at the moment it's shown, compulsion exists inasmuch as there's a danger of it not allowing the audience the freedom to see something, but just telling them what they *have* to see. It's evident that that's a latent danger that films have. The extreme form of that is in commercials or propaganda films, where everything is done to ensure the viewer gets a certain message. That's extreme manipulation, and manipulation is violence or duress.

Of course there are other films that show themselves to the viewer and leave him free to put the film together in his own way, and finally to determine which film he wants to see. Such films exist. And I try to get my films to be like that, so that they can exist in the imagination of each member of an audience, not forever pointing at something and saying; 'You're seeing this now, not something else!' 'That is the meaning of suchandsuch!' I try not to do too much finger-wagging and just leave the things there, so that you're free to see something or not, just as you are in life. That's not an easy thing to do, because the moment you start telling a story, you narrow your eye. And telling stories is partly such a problem for me because it tends to narrow down and simplify, to apply leading-strings or blinkers – either to the audience, or to what happens in the course of shooting.

From the danger of compulsion in a finished film, we can go on to talk about the use of force in the making of a film. There too manipulation remains a possibility. For instance, the manipulation of filming the ending first, then the beginning, and then the middle, or vice versa. That means that each day the actor comes on set, he only ever makes a little piece of the film, without ever understanding its function in the whole thing. That to me is a kind of violation. I try to avoid it whenever possible, because it does violence to myself too. I make all my films, with very occasional exceptions, in chronological order. The actors turn up on the first day, and we shoot the opening scene, and on the final day we shoot the last scene. It's the only way I really know of doing it. Every so often, there is a really compelling reason to upset chronology. And that's usually sufficiently traumatic.

And then a film being made often enough involves compulsion, as films can cost a lot of money, and are sometimes dependent on money. Money, to put it bluntly, can determine the contents of a film. Still more bluntly: all the money's there for is to turn a profit. As a director, I find myself on the victim's side, and I try to defend myself by – with the single exception of *Hammett* – being my own producer, and controlling all my own films. It can be an incredibly boring and sapping and stupid job that leaves me maybe 20 or 30 per cent of my energy for more creative work, but I do the other stuff to buy time. So no one can compel me to make cuts or force me to put in anything that doesn't fit my story. Getting the balance right between a story, a film and the money needed to make it is purely my own responsibility.

Often enough, it's the money that decides how close to its subject a film can get. There are films that cost a whole lot and still don't have enough, so they can never realize themselves. The relationship between money and ideas is a vexed one, because of the different interests. Now, I'm in the fortunate position – although I pay for it dearly – of at least being able to weigh up the competing interests *in myself*, and keep them in overall proportion.

*I remember what you wrote about directly experiencing that connection between money and films while you were making* Kings of the Road: *'At night, in some village hotel room, I would sometimes be overcome with terror. I would be sitting around, and it would be midnight, or two or four in the morning, and I still had no idea what we'd be shooting in the morning . . . and with fifteen people on the payroll! (. . .) So if I haven't managed to finish this page by morning, I'll be 3000 marks out of pocket.*

It really is a weird thing about films, the blatant connection between money and ideas. If a novelist is writing a novel, then maybe he has a publisher who rings him up once a fortnight to ask why the manuscript isn't ready yet, and there may be some financial interest somewhere in the background there, or he's been paid an advance for it or something – but it's still not that dominant; things like paper and typing ribbons aren't that expensive. And if I paint a picture and decide to paint it over, then that's purely my affair too.

But if I decide to shoot a scene again the next day because the sun happens to be shining, that has fairly sizeable consequences! That's the sword of Damocles that hangs over film-making; but it isn't just a negative thing, it's an asset in some ways too. It has a lot to do with the times we live in, and with the fact that films are a better document of these times than books or paintings are. A film is plunged into every kind of conflict, and not just on the level of subject-matter either, but because that's a condition of how it's made.

A film is something full of dangers for the person making it and the person watching it. Though if you know the dangers, you can use them too.

*That seems to me to happen in your films, and I'm surprised that it's even possible.*

It's not so surprising. I'm not the first to do it either. Right through cinema history there are people who produced their own films – starting with Buster Keaton, Charlie Chaplin or Griffith, to today where film-makers insist on having control of the means of production. And if you look at cinema history, you'll see a surprisingly large number of people who wrote while they were filming. When I explain how we made a film like *Kings of the Road* from one day to the next, never knowing where we'd be the next day and what we'd be shooting, it amazes people. But it really isn't such an uncommon way of doing it. Even in Hollywood there were a lot of people who brought along the script for the next scene on the morning of the shoot. There have always been these two sides, these two kinds of cinema: the purely industrial kind, no different than say the car industry, and the other sort with the blank sheet of paper, or the blank screen in the morning.

*How is it possible to keep an idea for a film going during all the fragmentedness of actual production? When you write or paint, everything is always available in front of you, you flick through pages you've done, or take a step backwards. But with a film you only get to see it once it's finished, after the editing –*

No, that's not the case. I think that what a novelist does, for instance, is an altogether riskier enterprise than making a film. You actually are able to see what you've done the following day. You're dealing with some very craft-related things, and so a lot of things are under your control: the framing of a shot, how you arrange a sequence, what you put into a shot and what you leave out, the lighting, the things people say to each other – all that has a lot to do with craft and expertise. An actor is a kind of craftsman, someone who for the most part has learned his trade; the cameraman is a craftsman who works with light. So you're working within a context of all these different techniques, and you can check them all the following day.

Of course a director needs to have some idea of the form he wants, or be able to introduce it as he goes along. But that seems to me much less impressive than a writer finding and using a literary form. Or a composer writing a symphony. Everything there seems to me much more fragmented and recalcitrant. With a symphony, you do only get to hear it when it gets performed. With a film, I get given a piece of it every day, I have people I can talk to or give instructions to, and who are guiding me all the time. Every day I can set the camera up in some place that gives me something, and I'm in continuous contact with reality, or exposed to a reality which also, so to speak, is feeding me, or sustaining me. There is always some landscape or city, a bird might fly through a shot, there's somebody standing in front of the camera, there are colours and shapes – there's always something. Compared to that, the formal control of a writer or composer is much more impressive than a film director's.

Sure it isn't easy, and there are tons of mistakes you can make. But it has a concreteness to it. And film is a kind of language too, with a fixed grammar.

*Back to violence. I had something slightly different in mind when I asked my question. I wanted you to talk about how a film compels the eye, regardless of content. Kafka says cinema impedes looking, films are like iron shutters in front of shops –*

I'm sure a film can get in the way of looking. It can make something visible, and just as well make it invisible. A film can really shut your eyes to things; a lot of films do just that. You come out of them, and you're blinded for days. Really! Gummed up. Other films, you come out of them, and you feel more open to the world than you did before.

*That's my experience of your films: they renew my pleasure in seeing.*

The director of a film uses his sight – his vision – on behalf of everyone who sees it. It's a huge responsibility. There's a chance you could equally be fitting everyone with your blinkers. It is amazingly complex, what a director does for other people. It's not just looking either, it's telling a story, it's playing music. You're doing all sorts of things at once. A film is a complex experience, in which looking is a big part of course, but so is listening, and feeling.

*The director in* The State of Things *says on the telephone: 'I'm at home nowhere, in no house, in no country.' And Marion in* Wings of Desire *says: 'I'm someone who's come from nowhere, who has no country, and I insist on that!' It's one of your themes which interests me a lot. What you've said about Nicholas Ray's characters, could equally well be applied to you: 'Wanting-to-be-at-home-but-belonging-elsewhere.'*

That's why Nick and I got along so well –

*Have your films changed in that regard? Has your life?*

When I look at it, I get the impression of something gradually becoming conscious; to begin with, it was self-sufficient – just movement, flight – and being on the road was enough by itself to make the world more bearable. You could see it in terms of a centrifugal force, I suppose, running away from a centre that you could maybe identify with 'home', and that movement alone being satisfying; but at that selfsame moment you start to think about what a return to the centre might be like. And by definition, travel has to be moving-toward-something as much as running-away-from-something.

In my first films I wasn't much interested in those contrary movements. But as it became clear to me why travel – why running-away-from-something – is so important to me, so the question arose whether it's possible to return, and whether returning might not actually be the whole point of going: getting some distance or perspective on something so as to be able to see it more clearly, or even see it at all.

*That's one of Hölderlin's central preoccupations; I don't know how well you know him –*

All I really know is his *Hyperion.*

*He always wanted to hymn 'something closely related to my fatherland or time', and to that end he consciously went via the alien, the Hellenistic, 'abroad'. I don't know if that applies to you too, whether you've now come back to Germany, or whether coming back to a particular place is even possible or desirable to you.*

Oh yes; desirable certainly. Desirable enough for me to want to make *Wings of Desire*, and arrive in this country I previously only ever wanted to get out of. Also to look at the country, and for the first time with a certain affection too. Which also means looking at my childhood for the first time.

But at the same time I can't accept that that means I've come home. On the contrary, I feel I've been here in Berlin for the past four years only in order to travel again, in a new way, with different interests and a different sort of delight. That means not being thrown out by the centrifugal force any more; also, not being intent on leaving somewhere, maybe more to aim to reach some new place.

The new thing I'm doing now is taking the idea of travel to new lengths, to a point where maybe the whole world starts to function as a single place. My new film is set in seventeen countries, beginning in Italy and going right round the world, visiting each continent, and finishing up back in Italy. It's going to be a science fiction film, because setting it slightly in the future, in the year 2000, – not all that far off – gives me a bit more imaginative freedom to deal with the present. There are things that I want to be possible in the present, which actually aren't quite at that point.

*Have you begun work on it yet?*

I'm writing it at the moment. Or rather, I've finished writing it. It's a story I wrote together with Solveig Dommartin, who's playing the lead in it. And now we need to travel like mad to get the whole thing set up.

*Would that be the sequel you announced at the end of* Wings of Desire?

No, not directly. *Wings of Desire* ends where it really ought to begin. The film is just a kind of prologue, the promise of a story to follow, a love story. And that's also why it says 'To be continued' at the end of it.

*And the 'nous sommes embarqués' alludes to this new travel film?*

That's right. It's a quote from Pascal by the way.

*The two concepts of 'story' and 'image' seem to be central to your thinking about films. You say somewhere that seeing is your profession, and stories are just a way of bringing in images. What makes images so important?*

What else can you show? Or: what other way of telling stories is there today? That means: how can you get something to move? I'm not a logical person, I can't establish a principle and derive things from that, not at all. The only way I have of moving something is if it actually moves. And then you look and see what it's rolling towards. And only in films, in a film's way with images, do I have something I feel I can work with. Maybe with music as well. But I'm not very musical. I'm more the visual type. Firstly, I have a good memory for images, and secondly I'm able to see images in my mind's eye before they exist in reality. I like seeing images too. If someone tells me something, it doesn't do much for me; what does it, is if they show me something. I expect at any other time in history I'd have become a painter, and it's just rather weird to me that I should be lucky enough now to be able to make films.

*Have you given up painting altogether?*

No, not altogether, but making films is such a complicated and absorbing business that I only get around to painting very occasionally, as a kind of hobby really.

Painting has become an object of wistfulness for me now. Each time I visit a painter in his studio I feel a pang. That would have been the alternative for me, and I've lost that now. But I know what I've lost it to. Still, I feel a kind of momentary regret each time. Painting seems like a wonderful life to me. Much preferable to writing. Occasionally, in the course of my work, I'm called upon to write something, and then I suffer the tortures of the damned. Writing for a living is unimaginable to me. There are no greater heroes for me than novelists. Writing is a terribly hazardous activity, and telling a story in words is far more fraught than it is in my own profession.

It's really not so bad in film, just because you do a little bit every day. It's like life. You find the hero for some story, put him in front of the camera, and something happens. The next day something else happens. And somehow you finish up with a story at the end of it. Or maybe just a set of circumstances. Storytelling in a film is continually nourished by the way you yourself and your crew just go from one situation to another. If you do your storytelling sitting behind a typewriter, you have to get it all out of yourself. That's truly heroic. And dangerous too. You have to be really careful, much more than if you're a film director, that you get enough living done, I think that's the greatest danger for people who purely write, that they don't have enough of a life themselves, or they take too much out of themselves, and then – that's why they're all on the bottle! Whereas as a film-maker you've always got lots of people around you, and there's a city or some landscape or something. You're always being given something. Of course, you need to give of yourself too, sometimes a hell of a lot – but you always get given something too.

*Something that cinema can do, and no other art-form, is to convey some sense of time. That first occurred to me when I saw Tarkovsky's* Mirror. *Would you agree that time is a big factor in films? Tarkovsky describes film as 'sculpting in time'.*

I think that's very true of his own films. It gets into metaphysics with him, because they are time-sculptures that change the idea of time. My films are just perfectly linear time-sculptures, because they keep on describing a way in relation to time; time in them is highly concrete. I use space as time, Tarkovsky uses time as space.

*It's also indicative that you began by finding it difficult to stop, to cut, to excerpt from time, and not show the entire process.*

That's a problem you're bound to have if you're a painter turned film-maker! My early films were just like paintings, only I used a camera. They were landscapes: the camera didn't move, nothing happened, no people walked through a shot, there was no dramatic action – they really were just like paintings that went on for a certain length of time. They looked at something and only stopped looking when the reel of film was finished. That was the only way I knew of ending something then. The idea of cutting was the first thing to really get me away from painting. Then I suddenly found myself in a different system of thought, a different type of expression. And even if I did gradually get used to the idea of cutting, and to the way that that gave you access to a new language that was less and less like the language of painting – I think I did always try to keep faith with time.

*In today's films, you get used to time passing very quickly, so I was quite astonished in* Kings of the Road *that there were all these scenes, and it was just one day in the story.*

That's because one's sense of time is terribly flexible and manipulable. But you're right. In *Kings of the Road*, time does pass very slowly, as the title suggests.*

*You keep coming back to the way directors like to 'kill off' characters in their films, saying it's just a story, while you feel a sense of responsibility towards them. The way you felt sufficiently responsible to Rüdiger Vogler to get him down off the top of the Zugspitze, where you'd left him at the end of your previous film,* False Movement –

*The German title, *Im Lauf der Zeit*, means *In the Course of Time* (Trans.).

Thank God I managed it!

*That strikes me as an unusually conscious way with art, so you don't mind breaking the frame in the interests of kind behaviour.*

I think that may have something to do with the way that films are really more to do with people, that actors in a film show themselves as people, not like they do on stage. On stage, an actor gets given a part to play. Stage continuity stresses the continuity of a part. So, although an actor may appear terribly open and vulnerable on stage, he's actually hiding behind his part the whole time. He *becomes* his part, so to speak.

It's the other way round in a film. In a film, he's exposed not to the audience, but to the camera, and only for short bursts, a matter of minutes in a day, and with the knowledge, each time, that if something goes wrong he'll generally get another chance at it. So in that sense he's not really exposed at all. In another way, though, he's far more exposed because he doesn't really have a part to hide behind. At least not in my films. Instead, he has to let himself be looked at, himself. And he has to learn how to show himself, be prepared simply to show himself.

It's a completely different proposition for the actor, and gives the director who puts it or 'exploits' it a new set of responsibilities. The actor is the same guy the moment after I switch off the camera as he was when I had it running. Whereas, when the curtain falls in the theatre, I can have a different conversation with the actor afterwards. That's the exciting thing about film, that you're dealing with the reality of people and things; that you get close to them as they really are, whereas in a play or a book you're, so to speak, always dealing with constructs. Or at least projecting constructs onto things. In a film, what gets projected afterwards is the thing itself, the man himself. All that gives you a completely new responsibility towards people and things, a responsibility that doesn't stop the moment the camera's switched off or the cut has been made. And that's especially true in the case of children, who appear quite a lot in my films. Then the film becomes this weird oscillation between form – an artform – and something that's pure life. You don't get that anywhere else.

*In* Nick's Film *you describe images that look 'so spic and span as though they'd been licked clean' as the product of fear: 'That's exactly what you go for when you're not sure what you want to show.' In Tarkovsky's last two films,* Nostalgia *and* The Sacrifice, *I have the sense that I'm just looking at gorgeous empty images. Because he wants to show something that lies beyond the senses, and he doesn't yet have the means to do it.*

Maybe they'll never exist either. That's the danger of film too, that you can make it appear as though there's more there than there actually is. I'm not saying that *at all* about Tarkovsky. Just that films in general find it very easy to 'dazzle', can claim to show something that they actually can't.

In fact, the better something looks in a film, the more wary you ought to be: you might be being deceived. And if you make a beautiful image yourself, you need to ask yourself each time what's justifying it, if it's just the shot and the beauty of it – which in a film is sometimes enough justification. But then you still need to check that you're not including something besides the beauty of the shot. In the context of a narrative, it can be terribly destructive putting in a shot for its own sweet sake, instead of helping the story. To vary the old proverb, you could say: 'Lies have beautiful legs.'*

In films with too many 'beautiful shots' in them, I tend to lose the thread or I get a sense that I'm not being told anything, or that there's nothing worth telling, and the beautiful shots are an attempt to distract me.

Occasionally, though – and this is where I think Tarkovsky comes in – when someone goes out into utterly new terrain where no one has ever been, and where there are a thousand pitfalls, like in *Stalker*, in the 'zone', where each step could be your last, where no connection holds, and there are no rules – then beautiful shots could be justified in a completely different way, as attempts to find *any* sort of form for the experience you want to talk about.

But how many films are there that go into the 'zone', that make you hold your breath because you're in such extreme danger at every step? Apart from Tarkovsky, very very few people in the last twenty years have done that, got into these life-threatening areas in film. Godard sometimes

---

*'*Lügen haben lange Beine*': 'Lies have long legs' (Trans.).

does it. Although he's so much of an old fox, I wonder if there isn't a bit of deception in that too.

*Tarkovsky's attempts to break into the spiritual –*

A film is always *terribly* available for that, and it's been exploited so many times too, to sell an instant mystical or mythical experience! I think that's probably too easy in films.

*Just because the appetite for the spiritual is so keen nowadays, it's apt to be exploited.*

And how! That's to do with the affinity between films and dreams. And out of that affinity, you usually get a mix of film and dream which is frankly a mess. One of the few to keep the distinction is Tarkovsky. Apart from that, when a film enters the terrain between dream and reality, metaphysics and reality, I tend to shudder and draw back, it's nearly always rot.

*For me* Solaris *was much more spiritual than* The Sacrifice.

I have to say I had the feeling in *Nostalgia* that Tarkovsky was using some of his typical narrative devices and shots as if they were between quotation marks. And on his sort of terrain, that's a dangerous thing to do. But it was only *Nostalgia* I felt that about. Not *The Sacrifice*. For me, that was another film where he really went out on a limb. The way he did in *Solaris*. For me, that remains his best film, that and *Stalker*. I think *Nostalgia* is a bit self-pitying, and that's hard for an audience. You can't easily forgive that. You can forgive mistakes, especially if someone's skating on such thin ice. But self-pity's a different matter. No one's free from it, in my own films I've slipped into self-pity from time to time – *The State of Things*, the first part is self-pitying. Not the ending, thank God.

*I remember you once quoted Kracauer: 'Perhaps the way today leads from the physical, and through the physical, to the spiritual.' In my opinion, that's true of your films. There's a sentence in early Steiner that's terribly important too: 'True human communion is the moment an idea becomes perceptible in reality.'*

Absolutely.

*In other words: if the spiritual is to be real, it can't be something vaguely otherworldly, it needs to be made visible in or through visible things.*

That's exactly what a film can do. It's actually the foundation for it. That's why film-making exists. Because that's what our century needed, a language that made things visible. And the most beautiful thing you can do in a film is a calm, quiet portrayal of something ordinary from which you grasp something quite universal. Like in all the films of Yasujiro Ozu.

*I'm afraid I don't know them.*

Oh, you're in for a treat! You have them all ahead of you.

*Your films have a lot of children in them, artless just like real children. Where does your feeling for children come from? Do you have children yourself?*

No. But that's often the way of it, that you can best describe what you most miss. In my films, children are present as the film's own fantasy, the eyes the film would like to see with. A view of the world that isn't opinionated, a purely ontological gaze. And only children really have that gaze. Sometimes in a film you can manage a gaze like a child's. Like the little boy at the end of *Kings of the Road*, sitting at the station, doing his homework. He's actually my dream of a film director. But the more you do, the less hope you have of coming close to your dream.

Children have a sort of admonitory function in my films: to remind you with what curiosity and lack of prejudice it is possible to look at the world.

*Berlin, 2 March 1988. First appearance in:* Individualität, Nr. 19,
*September 1988*

# The truth of images
## Two conversations with Peter W. Jansen

*I*

PETER W. JANSEN: *With your particular interests, gifts and possibilities, you could equally well have become a painter or writer. Why did you become a film director?*

WIM WENDERS: I might have been a lot of things. I might have got a degree in medicine or philosophy or God knows. I always thought I'd really like to be a painter. Most of my time now isn't taken up with making films, but with producing and a load of things I never even knew had anything to do with making films. At the same time, I have to say, I think that of all the things I like to do, like writing and taking photographs and painting, I don't think I could have put all those together in any better way than with film-making. Back in my early twenties, the time you happen into some career or other, it never even occurred to me, to be a film-maker, film director. I stumbled into it like a cow on a Sunday, no, that's not right, how does the proverb go?

*Did you have any models to follow?*

The first films I made were like paintings sustained over a certain length of time. I had more painter models than directors. Later on, I had some director models too, like Ozu, who made what so far as I was concerned were ideal films, who shows you the lost paradise of film-making. It wasn't till much later, after I'd begun to think of myself as a director, that I came across the German silent cinema, and came to admire those directors. But by then it was sort of too late for me to still have models.

*You once described Fritz Lang as a kind of father* manqúe *to you, even though Fritz Lang's films don't look anything like yours.*

They may look nothing like mine, but I still felt a great affinity with them,

I once saw them all in one go, at a retrospective in the States. Maybe it was because it was abroad, in America, and I saw them in pretty short order, but the whole of his life's work struck me as something utterly utterly new. If I'd known that as a young man, I would have said, yes, that's a point I could set out from. But I didn't know it then. It's a lost tradition so far as I'm concerned.

*For your generation of film-makers in Germany, there isn't any tradition though, is there? There are no fathers. And that's not just a topic for you personally, it's a topic in your films. I'm struck by how often in your films you get a father looking for his child or a child looking for its father, and while all other types of relationships are non-existent or malfunctioning, I got the impression that the relationship between father and child in your films is always lit by some optimism. Is that right?*

Yes, I'm sure it is. Maybe not just the father–child relationship, but the relationship a child can have with the world including, for example, its father. As I see children as models for seeing and thinking and feeling, perhaps I also see them as models for sustaining relationships.

*On the subject of children in your films, are they attempts on your part to shed light on your own childhood as well?*

Oh definitely, definitely. I think it's generally accepted nowadays that it's in childhood that the bulk of your personality is formed, and that stores of dreams and of sensibility come into being then too. And almost all the people I know who write or paint or make music, are drawing on those funds. The question is: how do you get at them? And how much do you just pretend you can get at them, and turn your childhood funds into a commodity? That happens, I know lots of example of that.

*Another theme of your films is restlessness or itchy feet. People are forever on the go, always looking for home. Have you come across the bit of Novalis that goes: 'Where does the secret path lead? It takes you home.' Would you see yourself as a Romantic, like Novalis?*

Yes. I think the great subject of the Romantic novel, of the *Entwicklungsroman*, is setting out into the unknown, and setting out into the unknown assumes, if you think about it, a return home at the end of it. Perhaps at the end of every search the thing you've been looking for in other places you end up finding in yourself. The whole idea of searching is a romantic subject.

*There's another clue that comes to mind: your films are full of images, perspectives, situations that remind me of Caspar David Friedrich. In many of his paintings Caspar David Friedrich shows the act of seeing, as you do in your films, where you keep referring to how seeing works or how people see. People keep opening windows and looking out of them. What's so great about seeing?*

The great thing about seeing for me is what distinguishes it from thinking, namely that it doesn't entail having an opinion. In thinking, every thought also contains an opinion of a thing or a person or a city or a landscape. There are no opinions in seeing; in seeing you can come to a view of another person, an object, the world, that doesn't imply an opinion, where you just confront the thing or person, take it on board, perceive it. I like the word insight. It suggests you can have truth and understanding just from seeing. Much more than from thinking, where you can lose yourself, or lose touch with the world. For me, seeing is immersing myself in the world, while thinking is distancing myself from it. As an intuitive type of person, seeing is my way of receiving impressions and of expressing myself.

*You once wrote that images in films don't necessarily lead anywhere else, they stand for themselves. Is that really the case? Surely in films, no image can stand for itself, because each image is read differently in the light of whatever image comes after it.*

Yes. By montage, by the unfolding narrative. But I still believe that montage and narrative are like great addition sums, and that if each image couldn't be taken on its own terms and at its own worth, the sum of all of them would amount to nothing. For me a story is a sum of individual circumstances, and each individual circumstance is so important to me that I'd happily see it by itself, and each image by itself. I think only if you give each image the right to be there for itself and tell its own story can you hope to be given the right by each image to place it in a sequence and make it part of some bigger whole.

*Couldn't it be that the story changes the image or images, maybe adding something which wasn't originally there?*

Stories are manipulation from beginning to end. And so images – I'll come back to this later – are more truthful than stories. Stories have a much greater capacity for lying. Images contain possible truths; if they're seen by children, a great many possible truths. Of course images are not hard to manipulate; here in Germany we know all about that. Look at German history. It's very clear from American cinema as well, the extent to which images can be manipulated. But for all that, images have a potential for truth, and stories for me are basically: tall tales.

*Is this an age hostile to images, as you've said, or an age of hostile images? Or is that the wrong question, because more and more images are being produced the whole time, and more and more images are shared around. Isn't the excess of images hostile to the individual image?*

Yes, and in my opinion that's one of the worst diseases of our civilization, being exposed to such an inflation of images. If you think of the nineteenth century we were just talking about: there were only painted pictures then. Some time photography came along, and of course print existed already, and so you had the reproduction of painted images, that was the next step. Then film images, and now electronic images as well. So that by now each one of us is exposed to such an overdose of images each day of his life that it seems almost anachronistic to say as I just said: images have a potential for truth. Of course, with the inflation in their numbers, each image has to contain less of the truth. In spite of that, I believe that the cinema, where it's so difficult to obtain each individual image, is a kind of last stronghold for that sense of an image I spoke about earlier.

*You began rather hesitantly as a director, with very basic forms that have been growing steadily more complicated. You've proceeded very cautiously, one step at a time, but you've also said that you found out how to direct only by doing it.*

Yes. At the beginning, I made images where nothing happened. There was no dialogue, no action, not even any people. It was just looking out of the window. Some time or other a couple of characters turned up and they appeared in shot, not close up, but in long shots, and one time they said something, but it wasn't really that important. The thing that mattered, back then, was the images. And then by and by I learned to trust the characters, and saw how from the sequence of shots and situations something like a story might result. And then some stories did come, and I began to realize what force there is in a story, what atavistic human force. So I learned to put my trust in stories.

*Which of the many parts of the film-making process interest you the most, and which less?*

I'm pretty much in dread of the very first part, which is writing, that's the most unpleasant. Then I like very much the bit where you're preparing a shoot, where you travel around looking for locations, meeting people, the stage when the film is just a kind of possibility in your head and keeps moving into new places and new possibilities. The actual shooting I hate like anything. It's the most ghastly stage of all, because there is so much compulsion and anxiety around, and because it's a huge waste of everyone's energies, my own and everyone who's participating in making the film. It's all so highly pressured. You need to get it done. It's such an expensive thing to do, to turn round and say: 'I'm out of ideas, I can't go on today.' You can just hear the money going down the drain. The actual filming really is the worst, I think almost every director would agree with that. Then I really enjoy cutting, that's my favourite stage really, the end bit, where you're on your own with the pictures, and putting together the film in the montage. For me that's paradise, the only time there's no anxiety.

*I've never come across anywhere in an essay or interview of yours where you've said anything about working with actors. Is that simply because it hasn't occurred to anyone to ask you about that?*

It must be because people haven't asked me. It's not because I don't have anything to say to my actors. It might also be because the actors I work with aren't so much actors as just themselves, in my films. I don't look to them to be actors, so much as to be themselves. For me a movie actor is someone who's prepared to contribute his whole self, not someone who's good at playing a part. In other words: the people I work with are usually people I knew previously, some of them well and for a long time, and that I like. Already at the idea stage, when I'm working on the script or thinking about the characters, I know who I want to appear in it, so that the actor and the part are somehow convergent, and the end result is that it becomes maybe less of a performance than might be the case in other people's films. Although that's also about the hardest thing to ask of an actor: to put in his whole person. Like the way that in *Paris, Texas* Harry Dean Stanton actually put the whole of his life story at the service of the film, so that we couldn't distinguish afterwards between Travis and Harry Dean Stanton. With Bruno (Ganz) and Otto (Sander) in *Wings of Desire* it was obviously a bit different. As angels, they weren't able to use their life stories in that kind of way!

*But in the case of Peter Falk, you worked out that he must have been an angel in some previous incarnation. Otherwise, you probably wouldn't have got him to be in the film.*

Yes, he was typecast!

*Werner Herzog once said his films come out of landscapes. Do you think one could say yours come out of cities? Are you more of a city director?*

Yes, I would think so. I really like cities. My first film was called *Silver City*, one of the next ones was *Summer in the City*, and then there was *Alice in the Cities* too – it can't just be coincidence. I have to say that by now I like empty landscapes like deserts and so on almost as much as cities. Then again, it's like opposites meeting, there are cityscapes that remind you of deserts.

*Could it be that cities are places where stories tend to collect more readily than landscapes? What about that as another point of departure for* Wings of Desire?

That began with me wanting to have Berlin in a film; the city called the film into being. For me different cities are like different people; some cities are open the way some people are, you want to get to know them, their strengths and weaknesses. There are cities that charm you, and others that are cold and remote. There are cities you have to be patient with, and cities that don't have much patience with the people who live in them. There are cities that are forever robbing you of your energy, just as there are people, and there are cities that are incredibly stimulating to your thoughts and your imagination. In many respects cities have their own character, so for me they become like having another star actor in a film. They're much more than backdrop or landscape: landscapes don't do so much for me.

*There are a couple of crisis points in your career, one after* The Scarlet Letter *and then, almost ten years later, another one after* Hammett. *After* The Scarlet Letter *you made* Alice in the Cities, *and after* Hammett, *or at the same time as* Hammett, Nick's Film *and* The State of Things. *Did making those films represent some kind of personal salvation for you?*

Yes, I think they did save me. At the same time, it was a bit of a gamble too. In each case, I was going for broke. *The Scarlet Letter* was such a disaster for me and my idea of what I should be doing in films that I thought afterwards, right, either you prove to yourself that it is possible to do something with films and with images and with stories, or you forget about it and become a painter, which is probably what you should have been doing all along. And it was just the same with *Hammett*; I thought, now you have to prove to yourself that there is independence and juice in what you're doing or else you should just let it go. The films I made after those setbacks helped me get back to a positive view of my work.

*Is it possible that both with* The Scarlet Letter *and* Hammett *there's a difficulty for you when the story or narrative takes precedence over images? When the story stand in this almost vampire-like relation to the images?*

That's right. I like the way you put it too. If I might put it slightly differently, at the moment when a story no longer gives you direct access to things themselves, to the actual people, the city, the objects around, when everything has a function and a set role to play, and the story becomes the single overriding consideration, then I feel like I'm in a vacuum. I can only really trust the story if I can trust the people and the things in it that might go to make up a story. But if it's the other way round, and the story is there first, and the story demands all my trust, then

I'm unable to do anything with it. That's what happened to me in *The Scarlet Letter*, and the same thing happened in *Hammett* too.

*That reminds me of a line in* The State of Things, *where someone says: stories only happen in stories. I suppose you could apply that to the present situation and say: interviews only happen in interviews. In real life there are no interviews, and in real life there are no movie plots. But does real life still exist?*

Real life only happens in real life. That's true, and I happen to believe that the cinema and real life are connected. I believe that cinema gets its ethics and its purpose by offering people help with their – real – lives, which means that it should have at least the possibility of relevance to life. Not all the time, that would be asking too much. It did once, early on in film history, and that's why I have this almost religious reverence for the films of Ozu, because I believe that in that golden age, his films always asserted a relationship with life. In early documentaries it's like that as well. If you look at Flaherty's films, for instance.

*You're on record as saying the cinema is closer to life than other art-forms. You could vary that and say the cinema is also closer to death than other art-forms. Truffaut said – and I think he got it from Cocteau – that making a film is like taking life. You've made a film about death yourself, about the dying of Nicholas Ray and, as I'm sure you know, there are people who distrust that film, who feel they're being made to be voyeurs at the death of an old sick man. Did you have doubts about that yourself while you were making it?*

I don't know if 'doubts' is the right word. We had to ask ourselves every time if it was all right to switch on the camera. It was never running without the question being aired, without a discussion, without agreement from Nick. The whole film is like one long answer to that question. It's not a self-justification, but a response to the question; and when we made the film and shot it and cut it and got it ready, then it was only because we thought, when the question came up, 'Can we do this? Is it all right to do this?' that the greater responsibility was to run the camera for Nick's sake, to give him the chance to be himself and to work, so that each time we made the decision together: this is right, this is proper, it's important for him to have us here, to have this work, to have a film crew around him during those last months of his life. That's the way he wants it. In any case it's better to have that than to have him lying in a hospital with the knowledge that his life . . . and the chance to work, is all at an end. The question was never off the table. And sometimes we didn't shoot, for instance when Nick had had to take too many painkillers and wasn't really in control. On those days we didn't shoot. Of course, that doesn't show up in the finished film.

*Your generation is the generation of '68. You lived in a commune, and some of your friends went the way of terrorism, some of them have been dead for many years. You kept yourself aloof, or you got out when violence appeared. But looking at your films, you don't see that reflected in any way, except in* Police Film. *Why is that?*

Films are always about what they're about and what they're not about. If there's something missing from a film, that makes it a part of the subject of a film. In my films, you don't get any sex or violence, because I think those are both things that can do a lot of damage. I only really like to show things that I like. I don't like to show something and then say, here is something I hate. The act of film-making, what you put up on a screen, is something you identify with, I think. That's how propaganda works. Because at that moment when you've got people sitting in a cinema and something appears on the big screen, there's automatically a kind of identification that takes place. You can't distance yourself from what you show. What you shoot, by implication, is what you support, it expresses what you want. That means that every act of violence, especially in American films that purport to be against violence, or war films that just pretend to be opposed . . . really every war film is a pro-war film. Every film with violence in it is a film in favour of violence. As far as politics goes, the most political decision you make is where you direct people's eyes. In other words: what you show people, day in day out, is political. Explicit political content in cinema is about the least political side of it, as far as I'm concerned. Entertainment is the height of politics. The most politically indoctrinating thing you can do to a human being is to show him, every day, that there can be no change. But by showing that something is open to change, you keep the idea of change alive. And that for me is the only political act of which cinema is capable: keeping the idea of change going. Not by calling for change. You achieve very little by that, I find. Maybe you need to do that sometimes, to call for change. But the really political act that cinema is capable of is making change possible, by implication, by not gumming up people's brains and eyes.

*To look at your output as a whole, from the very earliest to your most recent films, it seems you've evolved from terribly simple forms to images that are gradually becoming saturated with narrative, and with narratives that are getting ever more complicated. Does that development come from greater production possibilities, greater capacity to deal with the whole business of film-making, or is it that the world is becoming more complicated as you get older?*

The world is getting more complicated anyway. When you're doing something for the first time, say making a film, you have a particular kind of curiosity, a particular innocence and inventiveness, whereas if you're embarking on the adventure of making a film for the tenth time, you know a bit about what you're letting yourself in for, even though there are always new adventures ahead of you.

*What would you recommend to young people who are at that point today where you found yourself twenty years ago, when you were making* Alabama *and* Same Player Shoots Again?

I would say do everything! and do as much as possible, not just for yourselves. So, for example, watch as many films as you can, think about them, write down what you've seen, and if possible not just for yourself, but publish it too. That's the best way to learn, to see something and then to communicate your response to it. That's better than any film school; no film school allows you to do that. Be open to everything, that's the best training. Do everything, take pictures, think, write, travel, meet people, drink coffee.

2

To the End of the World *is a road movie, like almost all your films, and it's also a love story like – maybe – all your films, but in particular like* Paris,

Texas *and* Wings of Desire. *What prompted you to set this story in the future? Why science fiction?*

I wanted to be able to take a couple of liberties to do with themes that crop up in the film, to do with seeing and with images. And I wanted to take liberties with regard to travel as well. In the story there's this invention which is still rather futuristic: someone who is blind gets to see. And that seemed to me better pushed into the near future; in a film set in the year 2000 you might get away with a thing or two that you couldn't in a film set in 1991.

*There's also a new fascination of yours, the videotheque.*

Yes, that's right. Looking back, when you think what's happened in the course of the last ten, twenty years to do with our understanding of images and the way we deal with images, there's a generation around now, some in their teens already, that have grown up with these things – so I thought, extrapolating from that into the future, you can imagine how things might be in another ten years. I found that really interesting.

*But hitherto, you've always sounded rather cool about video technology. Was your film about Yohji Yamamoto,* Notes on Clothes and Cities *a kind of breakthrough for you, so far as video technology was concerned?*

Yes, it was a bit more than just playing around; I enjoyed it because I was able to do everything more or less by myself. It was a bit like a video toy. A while ago, maybe ten years now, there was an earlier form of video. We used it in *Nick's Film* with Nicholas Ray. When I look back on that, how cumbersome it was, how bad the picture was, how difficult to work with; the video element in the film struck me as a kind of cancer itself, and that was how we used it too, because it was a film about an illness, and the video pictures were like an illness within the film. Well, a lot has changed over the last ten years, an awful lot has changed. It's much easier to work with video, it's more practical, more democratic, anyone can use it pretty much any way he likes; and all those things to me are positive. I mean: they are useful. I'm not saying we should all suddenly stop making films, quite the opposite. Remember, with me the video only occurs in the context of film; it's rescued, if you like, or redeemed by putting it in a film.

If it was just video – if it didn't make it onto a film – . . . well, then I might not be interested in it at all.

*Video technology, especially in its new evolved form, HDTV, may have become a lot more flexible, have greater clarity and, even though I hesitate to say it, more honesty. But couldn't you argue that this easier and now sharper way of showing us what we see might be making sight too straightforward for us? Maybe with that type of seeing, the act of seeing itself is less conscious, and maybe we'll lose sight of the fact that the pictures we get shown are actually still only pictures?*

That's perfectly possible, it's one of the things my film is about; I believe, in fact, that seeing will be affected in that way. You can dig your heels in as much as you like, I think it's inevitable. Images have slipped into an inflation that's impossible to stop; on the contrary, it will grow stronger and stronger. And I think when we look back on 1991 from the year 2000, the way we're dealing with images now will appear pretty innocent. I think seeing will change, and all our dealings with pictures and images. That's why I was interested in making a film that looks ahead a little bit, and attempts to understand what lies in store for us.

*Of late, you've also used more technical tricks than in your earlier films, not just Schufftan's old mirror effect,\* but video tricks, using the new video technology. You've made images of a kind that were previously impossible, and images – I'm thinking of your dream-pictures here – that really only exist through that technology, and only in your film.*

Yes, because our film is set in the year 2000, and high resolution video pictures will be commonplace by then, I wanted to have them in our film too, and so, with the help of the Japanese state television channel NHK and the Sony corporation, we were able to work practically with prototypes and take certain tricks that you can already do on conventional video, and put them on high resolution tape for the first time and process them digitally, each image up to a hundred times, without the whole thing looking like porridge by the time we were finished. I don't think anyone else has done that yet.

\*Involving the unsilvering of part of a mirror.

*Can you explain that in layman's terms?*

The analogy with audio is probably the best. I guess most people probably know that it's possible to record a CD digitally, for instance, onto a digital tape, a DAT, which has forced the companies to introduce certain technical barriers because there is no qualitative difference between the digital copy and the original. And you can reproduce it a hundred thousand times, and it would *still* be every bit as good as the original. And now this is starting to happen with visual technology. An image that you store digitally can be processed – assuming all the processes are digital – and the second, the third and the hundredth generation of the image will still look identical, it won't have suffered any loss of quality. Now, with the film tricks we've had up until now, you have to work with intermediate negatives and intermediate positives, and each time, the picture gets worse, loses depth, loses contrast, becomes grainier. And that's why you can only do certain tricks on films; generally you try, if possible, to get them done in a single operation, so that the picture doesn't deteriorate too much, and we've used those traditional tricks too in our time, with mirror images and painting and so on. But after a couple of processings, you've done about all you can do, and the same is true really with video, traditional video. But if you store images digitally, you can perform as many manipulations of images as you want and more. There are some dream-images in the film that involved us in up to a hundred manipulations of the original image, without it looking like a blown-up bit of Super-8 by the time we were done with it.

*That comes down to a compression of time. Doesn't it then affect our whole sense of time and space?*

Yes, but basically every film does that anyway. Every film plays with time and space, and every cut and every process in a conventional film does that too. But I believe our sense of time and space has changed in the last ten to twenty years. We travel differently, we're accustomed to seeing differently, we see things much more quickly now. I've no doubt at all that an audience nowadays is much quicker to grasp things, and to grasp several things at once. Kids who have grown up with TV and with today's films are much quicker to get visual connections and can follow a story at a much quicker pace. I had that in mind too when I wanted to make a science fiction film, so we tell a great deal in a very compressed way. I thought, you can't make a science fiction film and act as though the language of images remains unchanged.

*Can pictures kill? In your film, you don't just show a blind woman seeing again; you show the blind mother practically dying from an overdose of images.*

Yes. Of course it's a metaphor, but I mean it very seriously. I think just as words can kill, so pictures have been able to for a long time as well.

*But when I look at your films – and not just your early work – there was always this delicacy and tenderness towards images. What's different now? If images can kill, isn't that a whole new philosophy? Have you had a change of mind, or of heart?*

No, I was only trying to take a hard realistic look at what's coming. I think the characters in my film are viewed with just as much tenderness as ever, and the blind woman, who dies from the images she sees, is shown with just as much tenderness as other characters of mine have in the past. But I was also trying to work out what's happening to us all, and to seeing *per se*. Seeing will certainly undergo a violent change, I'm quite convinced of that. I just tried to confront that as calmly and realistically as I could.

*What about dreams, though? Dreams becoming drugs, Claire and Sam getting hooked on their dreams. I was really astonished about you having these reservations about dreaming.*

Of course I don't have any reservations about dreaming as such, because that's a human impulse, and dreams are a source of energy and imagination for everyone who works creatively or imaginatively. As a kind of final twist in the film, I envisage people being able to re-view their dreams on monitors – the last stage of the abuse of images. That's depicted as a disease in the film, and that's the only way I can see it.

*The drug of their own dreams turns Claire and Sam into autistics. They weren't autistic before, and they won't be afterwards. So something has*

*happened. Have those characters – to go back to earlier films of yours – so
to speak caught the autism of Bloch in* The Goalkeeper's Fear of the
Penalty, *or of Wilhelm in* Wrong Movement? *Have you made a study of
autism?*

I have, in fact, but not in connection with that. Maybe autism isn't quite
the right term for what happens in the film, possibly only for certain
aspects of it. What actually happens to those characters is an overdose of
narcissism – which might come to the same thing. A narcissist is someone
who cuts himself off from the world, preferring to see his own picture to a
picture of the world. When I was making the film, I didn't use the word
autism, when I was explaining it to the actors; I just said that being able to
watch your own dreams is an act of extreme narcissism. And that that's
the drug. Of course their behaviour then is like that of autistic children,
they don't acknowledge the world outside, they just live inside themselves.
Other films of mine have dealt with that subject before: how affection or
love become impossible if you concentrate too hard on an image of
yourself or of someone else. That happened in *Paris, Texas,* where Travis,
the jealous guy, had too strong an image in his head of his young and
beautiful wife, which finally got in the way of his actually seeing her. And
I think the obverse of a love story – for me, anyway – is always that
problem when you don't see the other person any more, only the image
you have of him or her. Or, more fundamentally, when you fall in love
with an image – actually more of yourself than of the other person. That
moment where they fall into that autistic narcissim spells the end of their
love. Or it's the greatest danger they have to get through – far greater than
the thousand other dangers they had to get through to reach that point,
but all of them actually less threatening than that one.

*Can we go back to the subject of dreams. Dreams can be prophetic or
they can be buried memories. Is there a limit to what a human being can
encompass in terms of stories or memories? Among film directors I'm
thinking especially of Alain Resnais, who has worked with the contradictory imperatives of memory and forgetting. Does that interest you at
all?*

Films exist in that peculiar condition, where you can only experience a film – watch it if you're an audience, or make it, if you're a director or actor – in a kind of eternal present tense. In every scene you have to create something out of the present. You have to be there, and the greatest attribute of an actor is presence, being there, in front of the camera. But at the same time, in order to be fully present, an actor needs to be sustained by memories, for example; in other words, he needs to be able to draw on experiences and transplant them into that present, to make him really present and believable in a scene. As a director too, if you have an idea and you stand in a location, and there's scenery and some actors and a script and a story, and you want to make something out of all those ingredients – then you also need memory, you need to find something in the back of your mind that will bring some truth and some force to what you're trying to put on. But at the same time, if you're too much involved with the past, you can't make it into that continuous present that a film requires. It's a peculiar dilemma. You may get too bogged down in memories or the processing of memories, and then you lose your grip on the film's present tense. You end up making abstract, cerebral films. But sometimes you are able to relax completely in the present without switching off your memory, and those are the most fortunate films. Films exist in that crevice between past and present.

*Sam is healed by magic, Claire is healed when Eugene gives her his manuscript to read, a manuscript that tells her story, the story of the film. You could say she is healed by becoming aware of her own story. But it makes you wonder if it couldn't have been done equally well by pictures, conveying her story to her. But no, her story is conveyed to her by literature. I'd like to ask you once more: have you changed, is there now a stronger orientation in you, towards language, say?*

Quite possibly. Claire's sickness is a sickness of images, and she is healed by a much older and simpler art-form, by the art of storytelling, the art of the word. And Eugene, the writer who has followed and observed the course of her sickness, knows no other means of helping her, than holding up a mirror made out of words, not images. And it is these words that finally heal Claire, if I can put it so simply. When she reads her story, the sickness of the images is dispelled.

*So the sickness of images can't be cured by images – homeopathically?*

Maybe by very simple ones; I suppose it can. Sam's cure is shown in an abbreviated form in the film as it is at present. But part of it consisted of having him sitting in the landscape and drawing. Unfortunately, that had to be cut. He sat and drew rocks and blades of grass, and, like Eugene with his words, got back to a very simple atavistic and untechnological art-form. He sits there and does water-colours, and that's part of his cure. So, in our story, Sam actually is healed by images. The magic bit, him sleeping between the old people, was originally just one part of it.

*I'm tempted to connect the Eugene character with an early character in another film: is he a sort of variant on Wilhelm on* False Movement, *but whereas Wilhelm only wanted to be a poet, and almost found fulfilment in the mere wish, Eugene actually starts to write. Is that a 'right movement'?*

Yes, you could say so. I see Eugene as a writer who's really engaging with life.

*You aren't tempted to write a novel yourself?*

I don't know if I could. I don't think so. For the purposes of this film, I needed every means I could lay my hands on, pictures as well as writing, and I needed the figure of the writer to tell the story. And then I needed the musicians who collaborated on the film as well, because they too took the story forward. It's really such a complex and multi-layered thing, every kind of form had to be used. Whatever I do next is certain to be much, much simpler. Maybe I'll do something I've been wanting to do for ages, which is make a film with a cast of children. That would have to be told in a much more straightforward way.

*You didn't make the music for the film, but you commissioned it. How did that come about?*

Well, first there was just the idea that if I'm making a film set in the year 2000, it might be nice to have the odd bit of music on the car radio or something that isn't yet out. Music that for its part would also be slightly futuristic. I tried out the idea on two or three people, like David Byrne and the Talking Heads, and they wrote a song which appears on a video clip right at the start, and I liked that so much, getting a rock band to do something for the film and joining us in trying to look into the future, that by and by, and really only once we'd finished the shooting, we developed a concept for the music and ended up getting sixteen songs from sixteen different bands, all specially written for the film. Knowing the screenplay, the atmosphere of the film and the outline of the story, all of them latched onto a particular aspect of the science fiction story and made a song out of it.

*Had you thought about* To the End of the World *as a cartoon film?*

Ha, well maybe not exactly Mickey Mouse, but there are people making beautiful and complex and complicated cartoons, so it mightn't be beyond them to tell that kind of a story.

*'The point of films is to keep people from getting their eyes gummed up.' I'm quoting Wim Wenders.* To the End of the World *is awash with images. How come?*

I'm trying to see into the way we'll be dealing with images in the future. It's awash with images, because the future is going to deluge us with images. And I don't believe you can make a science fiction film while exercising a kind of puritanical reserve, sort of saying: at this point I'd like to distance myself from all this, and just make a very ascetic film about the future. If you did that, you'd be splitting off form and content, and, I think, refusing to face the future. I wanted to face it. I don't mean to say that I now believe I can only tell stories at that breakneck speed, and using such a flood of images. Quite the opposite. I think I'd really like to keep my next film very simple, but you can't project yourself into the future and at the same time say, oh, I'm not going to get into all this. You can't.

*Then let me quote you again. You say: 'You can't make films against something that aren't at the same time films that are for something.' That means if this film is a critical look at vision in the future, it has to be more than just critical.*

Yes, I stand by that. And you have to take that risk. Just as you can't make a war film that's anti-war, you can't make a science fiction film that's against the future.

*Not against the future. Against the way we'll deal with images in the future.*

Nor that either, sure. You can't make a film about dealing with images that insists that all images are holy. You can't make a film about that inflation, that flood, without being swept away in it yourself. It can't be done.

To the End of the World *is almost exactly the same length as* Kings of the Road, *but it seems longer to me. Could it be that it's not too long, but not long enough? That, unlike in* Kings of the Road, *you aren't given enough time and opportunity to identify with the characters and live with them?*

Yes, you don't get given a lot of opportunity. Things are always on the boil. At the end of *Kings of the Road*, you almost feel you've travelled the length of the East German border yourself, in real time, that's how slow it was. I think the new film has something like three or four times the number of shots in the same running time.

*So is the film too short?*

The film is told very quickly, that's true. It's cut in places, too. Maybe it is too short. You can only say that really if there's a long version to compare it to. I'm actually going to make one, but it's going to take me at least six months to do.

*How long is it going to be?*

I would say, maybe twice what it is now. The rough cut for a film is usually three to four hours, this one was ten. Then it was eight, then six, and when it was six I liked it a lot. There was everything in it that we'd shot, but it had a nice flow to it too. I wouldn't mind getting it back to six hours. Although it's a lot of work, especially with the soundtrack and all that. So it's going to take me a few months . . . Also because to get it down to three hours, we didn't just cut it very quickly, we also left out scenes altogether. The whole thing was such a mammoth undertaking over several years, I don't just want it put in mothballs, and that makes me keen on a longer version too. Though I don't know how a six-hour film will fare in the cinema. I suppose it will mainly be seen on television. Or maybe in a couple of cinemas too, with two intermissions or something.

*A theme in all your films is men and women not being able to live together satisfactorily. Maybe their parents could, like in* To the End of the World, *but then only because the woman gives up any claim to a separate existence of her own. At the end of* Wings of Desire *there was a ray of hope. But now it seems to have gone again.*

I wouldn't say that. I'm sure the love story in *To the End of the World* is a bigger and deeper thing than the relationship between the angel and the trapeze artist in *Wings of Desire*. The fact that love doesn't manage to escape the perils that surround it is just to do with the fact that the film is about those perils. But I don't think they make love impossible. The film points to some new dangers for love stories, and for men and women. But I think it can still be the way it looked at the end of *Wings of Desire*.

*There's a critical shot, a critical situation in the film that reminds me of the last shot in* Paris, Texas, *the shot of the family, or rather the union between mother and child, the picture that makes Sam burst into tears when he sees it again. Are family and union now all in the past?*

Maybe in comparison with the way it used to be, say, in the generation of our parents, or certainly our parents' parents – I think we've lost that. Perhaps that sort of family ideal is now over. The reality today looks very different to how it did in the last century or the early part of this one. Maybe it makes it more important and more rewarding too, that we didn't just chase after those old ideals and try to bring them back, but that we took a realistic situation of the kind you get nowadays, and tried to see what can be done with that. I don't know. It's possible that other cultural influences may come into play; in the area of sex, I'm sure the dawning realization of AIDS will change a great deal. It may end up producing such a profound change that maybe relationships will once again be more solidly built than they are now, or let's say than they were in the 1970s or 80s. What do I know!

*The men in your film don't manage to become friends either, they remain rivals. And the keenest rivals of all are father and son. There was a bit in* Kings of the Road *that dealt with rivalry between father and son, but it's much more acute now, with an incredibly hostile father who quite clearly doesn't love his son, and a son who badly wants to be loved by his father. All your films are films about you. Do you want to talk about your childhood?*

I think I had as happy and secure a childhood as it's possible to have. And I can assure you that the father played by Max von Sydow isn't based on my own in any way.

*But it's our generation's version of our fathers?*

It's certainly a version that's familiar to our generation. And I have experienced similar conflicts between fathers and sons, not with my own father, but between other people my age and their fathers.

*The child that plays such an important emotional and iconographic role in all your films, would you say that was more memory or appropriation?*

Memory, probably. Yes, definitely more memory.

*There are people who hold a rather different view of a child's psyche to yours. Where does your trust in children come from?*

From my experience of children. I've never felt my trust in a child has been misplaced. Also, looking back on my own childhood, I think I could trust my judgement as a child more than my grown-up judgement, and that's continually being borne out for me by my experiences with other children, whether they're aborigine children in the outback or German children – I've never felt my trust has been misplaced.

*The male friendships in your films – I'm thinking particularly of* Kings of the Road *and* The American Friend *– have from time to time been interpreted as latently homosexual. To* the End of the World *suggested something different to me, maybe it's absurd, but I wondered if Robert and Bruno in* Kings of the Road *and Jonathan and Ripley and* The American Friend, *and Sam and Eugene now might not each be two sides of one character. Two possibilities, say, or sets of contrasting aspects of one person . . .*

That doesn't seem too far-fetched to me. Whenever I look at my own output, I've always found it really hard to identify with two different characters at once. The simplest thing was always when there was just one person, like in *The Goalkeeper's Fear of the Penalty* or *False Movement*, or *Alice in the Cities* for that matter. Whenever there was more than one person, particularly if it was two men, like in *Kings of the Road* or *The American Friend*, it was difficult for me to split myself in two, so to speak. In telling the story, I tended to give the film's point of view to just one person; and it's through his eyes, if you like, that we see everything. So where there were two people, it seems quite possible that they might actually just be one and the same person. In the new film it's different, just because there are so many important characters in it, so there couldn't be just one perspective anyway; to some extent it's Claire's, seeing as the film begins and ends with her, and she's the heroine of the story. But she has half a dozen men characters around her, and none of them, I think, is quite Wim Wenders. Maybe Eugene, the narrator, because that's like me telling the story in the film.

*Were you able to identify with Bruno and Robert, or with Jonathan and Ripley at one and the same time?*

If you ask me who I like better, Bruno or Robert, I'd have a hard time telling you. When I run the film, sometimes I think it's one, sometimes the other, who has something of me in him, whether it's a bit of my experience, or my liking him. With Ripley and Jonathan it's a bit different, because Ripley's quite a mean character. Only because of the way Dennis Hopper played him, he became much more human and bearable than he is in the Highsmith books. But I think finally I'd see this or that side to Ripley and say, yes, all right, that seems familiar to me.

*Up until now, every film you've made has turned out utterly different to the one before it, even though your characteristic themes are present in all of them. And every film has put on a bit more complexity and difficulty. Is it possible for you to imagine that you might take a step or two in the other direction?*

I have to contradict you there. After *Paris, Texas* I made *Tokyo-Ga*, and after *Wings of Desire*, the *Notes on Clothes and Cities*. And after this latest film, which cost 23 million dollars, I definitely won't be making anything as expensive or complex or stressful.

*Fine, what about the one after then?*

The one after, give me a break!

*When you next make a narrative film, could you take . . .*

*. . . a backward step?*

*. . . a backward step.*

That's a difficult question. Looking at the work of my colleagues, it's clear to see it's something not many of them do – go back. It's so tempting to go on, isn't it? The means to make films – and I'm not just talking about money 'ut the means of artistic expression – are tempting; you want to push on and make further discoveries. But I think I can truthfully say that while I'll probably make a little documentary or something next, the film after that can't be a Sisyphean labour like this. I've got nothing planned anyway, no new projects up my sleeve.

*I'd like to ask you a very fundamental question about your work – at least it is fundamental for me and for some other people, perhaps it isn't for you. On the one hand, your films insist on the openness to interpretation of what is seen and heard in them. On the other hand, you're surely developing a complete system of signs in which, whether you like it or not, certain things acquire certain significance. Isn't there a contradiction there?*

Of course the openness to interpretation of things that you perceive with your senses is sheer utopia. But at the same time you need to insist on it, as a kind of utopia. If you can't hang on to it as an ideal, dream, utopia, whatever, then you lose your desire for it and your interest in it. And it's a cinematic ideal, telling a story purely through the senses. But as soon as you have a story – and with an epic story, it's still harder – you get that split. Storytelling itself is a cerebral undertaking. There's no getting round that. It's to do with proofs and dramaturgy, and very soon the ideal of a purely sensual narrative is just that: an ideal. But that's the force field in which every film has to exist.

*I can put my question another way. You revere Ozu, but the only sequence in* To the End of the World *that's at all reminiscent of him is the bit in the Japanese mountains, where you use Ozu's old actor too, Ryu Chishu. And what does he do in the story? You have him curing Sam, who is going blind; he gives him back his sight. That is: Ozu's healing force is being applied to Sam. Don't you think the Japanese betrayed Ozu, though, with their new video technology?*

I wouldn't say betrayed, because then you'd have to say the twenty-first century is bound to betray the twentieth and so on. But if that's your point of view, then betrayed would be right. But in that case we would all be betraying the art of photography, and before that the art of painting. Putting it baldly, all progress would be a form of betrayal. Now what Japan has been through in this century is astonishing, a people that are unquestionably quieter and more given to contemplation than their neighbours – and more than we are in Europe – turning themselves into a modern industrial nation, with images as their chief industry. It's hardly possible to buy a camera, whether a still camera or a video camera or shortly an electronic camera, that doesn't come from Japan, they practically have a monopoly. And even if you buy a traditional German camera, you open it up, and what's inside it is all Japanese made. At some stage, maybe in the 1950s, they got together and with incredible foresight worked out that the great industry of the twenty-first century was going to be images, and they set off deliberately in that direction. And when they did that, they really did put their history and traditions behind them.

*A fundamental contradiction in the market or in industry could also be a problem for the artist: each new product can establish itself only by denouncing or betraying or at the very least eclipsing its predecessor. But as an artist and a film-maker, you're surely interested in things being preserved. How do you see that contradiction or that conflict?*

The whole business of film-making is one enormous conflict. Because what other art is as closely tied to industry, is as subject to the rules and conditions that apply in that industry, simply because of the huge sums of money that are involved. In the film industry in the last ten or twenty years everything that was small has disappeared, everything that was slow-moving and meditative. It's just gone. There are still the old dinosaurs, so to speak, who still insist on doing things their way, without much success, of course, but at least they're still able to go on doing it. But for the majority of film-makers all over the world, the big question is how to make what they want to make, while following the rules that now apply. And by those new rules, no one can tell a story the way they did twenty years ago. By today's rules, Fassbinder would never have been able to make forty films. And Ozu wouldn't have been able to make one.

*You mention Fassbinder – he once said that 'take'\* isn't just a film term, but a moral category . . .*

Unfortunately, you only get that double sense in German.

*But you still get it. How would you describe your morality as a director?*

The two senses of 'take', what you set up and shoot, and the attitude of whoever is shooting and seeing whether it 'takes' – I would say that the morality, the moral act in every 'take', is determined by the 'take' on things of the person in charge, and for me that comes down to respect. Respect for what is in front of the camera, in the shot, and what, as truthfully as possible, should be saved and projected onto the screen at the end. That saving I think you can only describe as a form of respect. You try to respect what's there, and to preserve its truth. Maybe not everyone will want to believe me; but I believe that each 'take' in a film also makes visible the 'take' on things of the man or woman who is responsible for it. Each 'take' shows you what's in front of the camera but also what's behind it. For me a camera is an instrument that works in two directions. It shows both object and subject. That's why in the end each 'take' shows the 'take' of the director. It's a truly amazing side of film-making. Unfortunately, you can only really do it in German. It was there, in the word, before it was ever applied to films. It's a good language.

*Conducted and recorded for 1 PLUS on 1 April 1989 in Berlin (1) and on 18 August 1991 in Munich (2)*

---

\* The German word is 'Einstellung', a 'shot' or an 'attitude' (Trans.).

# The dubious revolution
Conversation with Peter Buchka on the possibilities
of digital images

PETER BUCHKA: *Mr Wenders, your new film* Notes on Clothes and Cities, *with and about the Japanese fashion designer, Yohji Yamamoto, comes into your category of 'diary-films', filmed essays in which you refine and redefine your aesthetic positions. What interested you about Yohji Yamamoto?*

WIM WENDERS: It came about because I wanted to think about the future in a playful, experimental sort of way. I was still busy with the scripts and preparations for *To the End of the World,* an important part of which was trying to imagine how the world might look in 1999, how the cinema will look, and electronic language, and how it is now . . . How it is that there are some very clear trends around now; certain things are gaining in importance that no one was taking seriously ten years ago, never mind twenty, and one of them is fashion. In my projection forward to 1999 that's very important. Fashion takes a much bigger place in my notion of 1999 than it has now, I see people getting into it more and more, becoming more and more dependent on it, more and more consumption-orientated.

*But you're not interested in Yamamoto's designs in the film.*

Did you look? You see them the whole time.

*My impression was that Yamamoto only interests you as an artist of a similar type to yourself, someone who tries to accommodate everything into his own vision. You seemed to me to be impressed by the* way *he does things, rather than by* what *he does.*

No, no; I am interested in what he does, and it shows too in the film. Only: he's doing something different now, when I'm showing my film, than he was doing then, when I was shooting it. His field is fashion, and to show each new fashion and to take a terribly serious view of it would be to turn my film into a kind of 'victim of fashion'. Because by the time the film comes out, Yohji will be into something else again. He'll be another three or six collections further on. In other words, he can't be tied down to whatever he was designing and I was filming in 1988. So I am interested in the *what*, but not so much as to want to saddle him and me with it for good.

*But you begin on this high, almost philosophical note, with a reflection on identity. And part of identity is surely what a person has achieved in the past. Surely you wouldn't want to deny the films you made twenty years ago?*

No, but I wouldn't make them in the same way now. He doesn't design in the same way either, above all his ideas on men and women have changed in the past twenty years. In addition – and this actually troubled me far more than I let on in the film – he doesn't keep anything. He's quite ruthless about burning everything he doesn't sell. I have my negatives, but he keeps going forward all the time. He has no collections or 'archives' of his earlier designs.

*But surely that's something that you absolutely don't share with him: that combination of identity and irresponsibility.*

Film-making is a far more moralizing thing than making clothes. It involves moral decisions all the time – maybe it comes down to that. Then again: the film puts in question my understanding of form, quite radically, because I agreed to make it in video. And not like in *Lightning over Water*, when I used video as a kind of . . .

*. . . death-image . . .*

. . . no, as a kind of cancer within the film itself. Instead, on a trial basis, as it were, I made myself take it seriously, and, to my astonishment, found myself enjoying it. And that's why I now believe you can use it in a serious way – in spite of the way I've inveighed against it in the past.

*One thing puzzles me in the film, the way you cheerfully adopt something you've always detested in the past: a tourist's perspective. Your commentary still expresses a few reservations, but the (video) pictures are absolutely that.*

I took the plunge, didn't I. I noticed that in that enemy language, things can be expressed that escape film. That escape film because the roots of film are in the previous century, because it's a very difficult, form-conscious language. The revolution we're experiencing today is like the invention of the printing press. The leap from photographic image to digital information really is a revolution: the risk is that film just stands there gawping with its mouth open, and misses the connection.

Hence the 'tourist's perspective'. Tentatively, almost reluctantly, I made myself go out and experiment. I wanted to have a look: what's there to see?

A television image, you know, 'writes itself', it's not a solid image, it's built up line by line on the screen. So I tried to make a film to read 'between the lines', if you like.

*So, by that token, each of the various types of visual reproduction has its own specific aesthetic value?*

By virtue of production conditions, the way it's processed and so on, the language of film is a mighty form, one that imposes itself on everything that appears in it and through it: every object, every landscape, every face. Video isn't like that. Film has a kind of innate sense of form that video doesn't have. It can't do it, doesn't want it, doesn't need it. It represents a kind of democratic dilettantism: anyone can do it, anyone may do it, who gives a shit.

Now, on the one hand, that leads to sheer randomness; but, on the other – because the innate sense of form is absent – it has the potential to capture reality in a different way: more quickly, more spontaneously, on occasion even more genuinely, precisely because of the absence of form, and of film grammar.

*The formal equivalent of irresponsibility, in other words.*

There is something 'irresponsible' about video, and that makes it very suitable for the subject I was investigating, namely fashion. Film images of mine on fashion were like an assertion, a Procrustean way of 'saying something' on the subject. Video is a much more appropriate way of approaching the subject, because it's content merely to 'show' something.

*All the same, you begin with this lofty discussion of identity. And you end on another high note, with the idea of authorship; the shot of an army of bustling dwarves, all going about doing Mr Yamamoto's bidding.*

The question of identity arises quite naturally from the conflict between the two languages of film and video. If you film something and video it, what you get is two completely different ways of seeing and experiencing it, like the difference between an original and a copy. Now if you accept – for all our old attachment to the cinema – that infinitely more people watch videos these days than go out and see films, if you take that as a given, and if you accept the projection of how things will be in ten years' time, say, then it seems to me you've got to put an end to the deadly enmity between the two, and accept video as a language.

*So you think video will one day be able to generate a serious film-language of its own?*

Absolutely! You have to hope so for the sake of mankind. You *have* to assume that it will one day happen. Otherwise, it could be the great cultural calamity of the next century, if it failed to become a language and merely remained an idiot box. What a catastrophe!

Only it would be wrong to take it too seriously just yet, say in my Yamamoto film. I just use video as an intermediate phase; everything I shot in video that pleased me, I then put on film. I rescued my 'video' by putting it on 'film'. I would never ever use video that had to remain video.

*So tell me, what advantages does High Definition have over present-day technology? It can't just come down to having twice the number of lines in a picture, higher resolution, or the undeniable brilliance of the image?*

It's the transition from photography to digital information! The moment you make a digital recording of a television picture, the picture becomes indefinitely reproducible, without any loss of quality, and infinitely manipulable. You'll never know what was ever true about the picture.

I've just spent three weeks in Tokyo working on High Definition. We were the first foreigners who were allowed to work with that medium and that technology at NHK. For me, it was like being brainwashed! As a film-maker you're used to accepting what you've got on the cutting table as reality. That's it! OK! But with a digitally recorded image, you can do anything you like, and no one will ever be able to say, 'That's not right! There should be a house standing there.' Abracadabra, five minutes later the house is gone as though it had never been. The information 'house' has been deleted.

*Is that really any different from the computer tricks you get, say, in* Star Wars?

Those tricks you can follow and trace stage by stage. There are six intermediate positives, where you can see exactly how it's done. In digital video there aren't any intermediate stages. There is no original. There are no negatives either, that would allow you to say: Hang on, look, it used to be this way before, and now you've gone and done such and such. With digital recordings that's finished. You can fiddle with a film-negative, but the expectation of truth that you bring to the image still demands to be satisfied. Not in digital TV. The image has no necessary relation to the truth any more.

*That's the dream of propagandists everywhere. When Stalin had Trotsky airbrushed out, you could tell.*

Not any more, Trotsky's feet have disappeared along with the rest of him.

*That would be an utterly new quality . . .*

There's no relying on anything any more. You work with a medium that's no longer subject to any notion of truth or accuracy, where all that matters is what you do with it – and you can do *anything* with it.

*Originally appeared:* Süddeutsche Zeitung, *28 March 1990*

## High definition
Talk given to the IECF Round Table Discussion on the subject 'Can HDTV make creators' dreams come true?'

I wish you all a good morning, this beautiful autumn day. The question before us today is: 'Can artists and film-makers realize their dreams with High Definition Video?'

My dreams and my nightmares are not just a part of my life as an 'artist', they are just as much part of my day-to-day life as a human being, as with any one of you. You all work in video, much more than I do. But as you know, I'm a film-maker first and foremost, and it's as such that I've been asked to speak to you. Before I set out my view of High Definition, let me first tell you about my relationship with video.

'Video', I seem to remember from my schooldays, was originally a Latin word. For a couple of thousand years, its meaning was 'I see', and only very recently has it been used as a term for an electronic image.

As a film-maker and photographer, seeing is my profession, if you like, my handiwork. And, growing up among photographic images, video – the electronic recording of images – and television – the transmitting and receiving of such images – generally left me cold, compared to film and photography. To be frank, as far as I was concerned, video didn't mean 'I see', but more like 'I can't see', or at least 'I can't see too well'.

Of course, with video you can cut production costs and time, but even that has only limited appeal to me. Better vision matters more to me than cheaper or faster vision – especially nowadays, when all of us are inundated with images from all sides, night and day. I would rather see less often, but properly. In my eyes, a few clear and precise, even truthful images count for more than innumerable mediocre ones.

It was the name that first got me interested in High Definition Video. Initially, it struck me as a contradiction in terms: video on the one hand, and high definition on the other – surely not?

Then, during the last year, and thanks to the generosity of NHK and Sony, I was allowed the opportunity and the privilege of working with the new medium of High Definition in the studios of NHK, with their technical assistance, and of using it to make part of my new film, together with my assistant Sean Naughton.

My experience in the course of that year has changed my position towards video. I am now prepared to believe that the electronic medium can become an adequate tool for seeing and showing. The electronic image is finally able to represent an object faithfully, without coming up against the all too glaring limitations of having four hundred lines or eight hundred lines in a picture. It strikes me as a quantum leap which, I would assume, will lead to the full maturation of video and television. At long last, video and television will be able to live up to the original meanings of their names.

But, and I am coming to what I really want to say to you this morning, so put it in block capitals: BUT is it enough that High Definition is technically in a position to see the world and to record and reflect it more truly and more accurately? I'd like to throw out a few questions to which I'm not remotely in a position to give answers myself; I think that's the point of our get-together: to throw out questions, and discuss problems. The time for answers is probably yet to come, in any case. High Definition is still at an early stage of development, and is only just beginning to become available to a wider public.

To some of you, who work much more closely with television and video than I do, a few of the thoughts and questions I want to put before you may therefore sound rather polemical. For instance: it always seemed to me a crass cultural error that video – old-fashioned, conventional video – should have supplanted and largely destroyed the original art of telling stories in pictures – the cinema – before it was fit or ready to do so.

The electronic image has developed a language of its own; a much simpler and cruder one, admittedly, than the elegant and organically evolved one of cinema. It is conditioned largely by its limitations. For instance, because of its own want of clarity and resolution of image, television has eliminated the long-shot, which so beautifully conforms to the human eye, and replaced it with the tedium of close-ups. The standard electronic image is the 'talking head'. And chiefly because of the competition between television stations, television has instituted a faster rhythm of cutting and simpler dramaturgic structures in order to hold on to its share of the audience.

With these means, and others, television has affected two or even three generations of children who have grown up with it, and who now have no use for a panoramic view or a gentle pace. The close ties between television and advertising have also done much to shape – and deform – the language of television.

In short: video culture has undermined and largely destroyed its predecessor's language. Films nowadays look almost indistinguishable from television productions anyway, as their exploitation increasingly happens on television, where the audience is so accustomed to TV pictures that it now expects them even in films.

I'm not the first person to say this: television has replaced cinema by something inferior; it has replaced cinema too quickly and too greedily – and without being well enough equipped to mount a proper challenge. If this is how it is, what I'd like to know is: will the new High Definition electronic medium only replace the old electronic images while keeping the same impoverished language, or will the 'electronic cinema' try and reverse the damage and the injustice that was done to the previous image-culture – the cinema?

High Definition, in place of 'low' definition, has the historic opportunity of correcting bad habits of seeing, and to come up with a less terrorist, and a kindlier, more human way of seeing. Because in the end, High Definition won't be justified by technical improvements – technology is always improving, in all fields. No, 'High Vision' will one day be judged for its moral effect on vision, not for mere technical progress.

Please don't get me wrong, I'm not one of those moralists who believe that we or anyone else can have much say over what ends up being available on High Definition video cassettes or on High Definition TV programmes. There are bound to be High Definition porn films; no one will be able to stop that from happening. But that's not what I'm talking about. I'm talking about the way the new medium will ultimately answer to the human need to see and to be informed about the world, how it will tell us stories and entertain us.

In any case, I have great hopes that High Vision will evolve a less cynical language than its predecessor. And, as a film-maker myself, I'd like to pass on a word of advice: image-makers and producers working in

High Definition should try to learn from a better source and a better tradition than television. They should try to learn from the far more expressive and civilized language of the cinema. High Definition is still a very young culture; what we are presently experiencing is its youth, maybe its adolescence. It's easier to learn when you're young. The older you are, the more you're a prisoner of your bad habits of seeing.

So I'm hoping for a culture of 'High Vision' that won't get into bad habits right from the start. I'm hoping, for instance, that the new picture format will permit the reintroduction of the long-shot, and that aesthetic considerations will once again be applied beyond merely how best to exploit the eyes and brains of human beings.

Another point I'd like to raise concerns the new medium's relationship to reality. That too could well turn out to be a moral issue. We all know how much the era of the digital storage of information has affected the notions of 'original' and 'reality'. And after spending some time at NHK, working on my 'dream sequences', I know how much electronic images, especially digital ones, can be manipulated. You know all that, this isn't news to you. The electronic image, in particular the High Definition image, is already an abstraction of reality. The individual image no longer exists, and there is a vast and complicated technology between the eye looking through the camera and the world in front of the camera. The permanent and palpable image no longer exists.

Between the recording and the reception of an electronic image, there is an enormous loss of 'reality', which makes it all the less surprising that the TV picture has so little regard for 'reality'. This again is a huge subject, and I've only broached it in order to put forward a thought: that High Vision could balance the loss of reality by the gain in image resolution. The loss of reality is a serious affliction for civilizaton. It is a virus for which there is no cure, if indeed anyone has even attempted to find one. It's more destructive of life than any other virus.

High Vision, and this is my dream, could help to sharpen our sense of reality; my nightmare is if High Definition in the long run only continues to undermine any remaining faith we may have in the truth of images.

It's clear that the future of entertainment lies with High Definition – storytelling, news, reportage, it is what our children and our children's children will be used to seeing. In twenty years' time we'll look back at our present television sets with the same pitying smile with which we now look back at our black and white sets from the 1960s. But whether High Definition will bring a real improvement to our lives and our children's lives, that is now up to us.

I'm an optimist by nature. Here, then, is a new technology which is still looking for a language of its own. Creative people all over the world should start working with it, and using it and improving it – yes, maybe try and shape it from the start. If artists or 'image-craftsmen' don't take the tool in their own hands, and refuse to help shape the medium, they will have only themselves to blame if, in future years, High Definition doesn't correspond to their vision.

I used High Definition in my own film because it is about dreams. In the course of my work on it, I watched all the dream sequences in the history of cinema, and found that not one of them was like a dream; all of them looked like films. And while I was thinking about what dreams really look like, I hit upon the idea of using High Vision technology. I was astounded by its possibilities. They put me in the position of being able to devise a language (and we're still working on it as I speak) that we could never have done using cinematic means.

Some of our High Vision dream images consist of as many as a hundred different layers, one image superimposed over another, in a way that, as you know, would be impossible with film. Even if you worked through just ten duplicated negatives in succession, you wouldn't be able to come up with a decent picture.

But, to get back to the original question: 'Can High Definition television make creators' dreams come true?' I could have saved you a lot of time and said: Yes, it can. And will it? We'll see about that.

Thank you for listening.

*Tokyo 5 November 1990. Retranslated from the English [and then from the German! Trans.].*

PART III

# Notebook on Clothes and Cities
## (English commentary)

We live in the cities.
The cities live in us . . .
time passes.
We move from one city to another,
from one country to another.
We change languages,
we change habits,
we change opinions,
we change clothes,
we change everything.
Everything changes. And fast.
Images above all,

change faster and faster, and they have been multiplying
at a hellish rate ever since the explosion that unleashed the
electronic images; the very images which are now replacing
photography.

We have learned to trust the photographic image.
Can we trust the electronic image?
With painting everything was simple:
the original was unique and each copy was a copy, a
forgery.
With photography and then film it began to get complicated:
the original was a negative, without a print it did not
exist, just the opposite . . . each copy was the original.
But now, with the electronic image and soon the digital,
there is no more negative and no more positive.
The very notion of the 'original' is obsolete. Everything

is copy.
All distinctions have become arbitrary.
No wonder the idea of identity finds itself in such a
feeble state.
Identity is OUT! Out of fashion. Exactly.
Then what is in vogue if not fashion itself?
By definition, fashion is always IN.


*I*

You live wherever you live,
you do whatever work you do,
you talk however you talk,
you eat whatever you eat,
you wear whatever clothes you wear,
you look at whatever images you see . . .

YOU'RE LIVING HOWEVER YOU CAN.
YOU ARE WHOEVER YOU ARE.

'Identity' . . .
of a person,
of a thing,
of a place.

'Identity'.
The word itself gives me shivers.
It rings of calm, comfort, contentedness.
What is it, identity?
To know where you belong?
To know your self worth?
To know who you are?
How do you recognize identity?
We are creating an image of ourselves,
we are attempting to resemble this image . . .
Is that what we call identity?
The accord

between the image we have created of ourselves
and . . . ourselves?
Just who is that, 'ourselves'?
'Identity' and 'fashion': are the two contradictory?
'Fashion. I'll have nothing of it.'
At least that was my first reaction when the Centre Georges
Pompidou in Paris asked me to make a short film 'in the
context of fashion'.
'The world of fashion. I'm interested in the world, not in
fashion . . .'
But maybe I was too quick to put down fashion.
Why not look at it without prejudice?
Why not examine it like any other industry, like the movies
for example?
Maybe fashion and cinema had something in common.
And something else: this film would give me the opportunity
to meet someone who had already aroused my curiosity,
someone who worked in Tokyo.

2

Film-making . . . should just remain a way of life sometimes,
like taking a walk, reading a newspaper, eating, writing
notes, driving a car . . . or shooting this film here, for
instance, made from day to day,
carried along by nothing other than its curiosity:
a notebook on cities and clothes.

3

My first encounter with Yohji Yamamoto was, in a way, an
experience of identity:
I bought a shirt and a jacket.
You know the feeling . . . you put on new clothes, you look
at yourself in the mirror, you're content, excited about
your new skin.

But with this shirt and this jacket, it was different.
From the beginning they were NEW and OLD at the same time.
In the mirror I saw ME, of course, only better: more 'me'
than before.
And I had the strangest sensation: I was wearing, I had no
other words for it, I was wearing THE SHIRT ITSELF and THE
JACKET ITSELF: And in them, I was MYSELF . . .
I felt protected like a knight in his armour.
By what? By a shirt and a jacket?
I was flattered.
The label said 'Yohji Yamamoto'.
Who was he? What secret had he discovered, this Yamamoto?
A shape, a cut, a fabric?
None of these explained what I felt.
It came from further away, from deeper. It came from the past.
This jacket reminded me of my childhood, and of my father,
as if the essence of this memory were tailored into it, not
in the details, rather woven into the cloth itself.
The jacket was a direct translation of this feeling, and it
expressed 'father' better than words.
What did Yamamoto know about me, about everybody?
I went to visit him in Tokyo.


4

Yohji's Tokyo office was brimming with photos and images,
stuck to the walls and scattered about his work table, and
the shelves were crowded with photo books, among which I
discovered one that I knew and treasured as much as he:
*Citizens of the Twentieth Century* by August Sander.


5

I believe this photo of a young gypsy was Yohji's favourite
in the book.
Not simply for what he was wearing, rather for the forlorn

look in his eyes and the way he stuck his hand into his
pocket.

6

Tokyo is a long way from Europe. European clothing has only
been accepted here for about a century.
If, on my first encounter with Yohji I had been amazed by
the history locked into a shirt and a jacket and the
protection they had offered me, I was indeed more amazed to
see the effect of his work on Solveig.
She had worn dresses by Yohji for some time already and
each time they seemed to have transformed her. As if by
slipping into these dresses she had slipped into a new part
in an altogether new play.
So when I went to Tokyo to film Yohji in his studio as he
was doing the fittings for his new summer collection,
I was most curious about his rapport with women.

7

When you don't understand somebody else's craft the first
questions are usually very simple:
Where does your work begin?
What's the first step you take?

8

Form and material.
Same old dilemma, same ritual as any other craft:
stand back, look, approach again, grasp, feel, hesitate,
then sudden activity, and then, another long pause.
After a while, I began to see a certain paradox in Yohji's work.
What he creates is necessarily ephemeral, victim to the
immediate and voracious consumption, which is the rule of
his game.

After all, fashion is about 'here and now'. It only deals
with 'today' and never yesterday.
By the same token, Yohji was inspired by the photographs of
another time and by the workclothes of an era when people
lived by a different rhythm, and when 'work' had a
different sense of dignity.
So it seemed to me that Yohji expressed himself in two
languages simultaneously. He played two instruments at the
same time:
the fluid and the solid,
the fleeting and the permanent,
the fugitive and the stable.


9

Me too, I felt like some monster making this film,
working like him in two different languages and using two
essentially different systems.
Behind my little 35 mm movie camera, I felt as though I were
manipulating something ancient,
or perhaps 'classic'. Yes. That's the word.
Because my camera only takes 30-metre rolls of film, I was
obliged to reload every 60 seconds.
Therefore I found myself more often behind my video camera,
which was always ready and allowed me to capture Yohji's
work in real time.
Its language was not 'classic', rather practical and
efficient.
The video images even felt more accurate sometimes, as if
they had a better understanding of the phenomena before the
lens, as if they had a certain affinity with fashion.


10

My little old Eyemo. You have to wind her by hand,
and she sounds like a sewing machine. She knows about

waiting, too.
Night fell.
Yohji did not stop working for one second.
One dress followed another.
Later on, most of them would be made of black materials.
I asked what black meant to him.


I I

Slowly, and almost in spite of myself, I began to appreciate
working with the video camera.
With the Eyemo, I always felt like an intruder.
She made too much of an impression.
The video camera impressed and disturbed no one.
She was just there.


I 2

On the way to the courtyard of the Louvre, where the
fashion show would take place the following day,
we happened to encounter this young Japanese woman on the
Pont des Arts, dressed in clothes by Yohji.
In the turmoil of rehearsals, he remained a monument of
calm . . .


I 3

The direction, well, nobody seemed to know it except Yohji.
At least that was the impression I got in the chaotic
atmosphere of the Paris studio the night before the show.
Actually it had the mood of an editing room just before
finishing a first cut.
In effect, that is exactly what Yohji did that night:
he established a montage and the proper series of scenes
and images for tomorrow's show.

## *14*

When I visited Yohji in Tokyo for the second time, he was
preparing the reopening of one of his shops that had just
been renovated.
It turned out that the most difficult part of the process
was the signing.
When your signature has become a trademark, then you have
to reproduce, in this one gesture, and each time anew, what
you are all about.

## *15*

In Japanese, the name Yamamoto means:
at the foot of the mountain.

## *16*

All of a sudden, on the turbulent streets of Tokyo, I
realized that a valid image of this city might very well be
an electronic one and not only my 'sacred' celluloid
images.
In its own language, the video camera was capturing this
city in an appropriate way. I was shocked:
a language of images was not the privilege of cinema.
Wasn't it necessary then to re-evaluate everything?
All notions of identity, of language, images, authorship . . .
Perhaps our future authors were the makers of commercials,
or video clips, or the designers of electronic games and
computer programs . . .
Holy shit . . .

## *17*

And movies?
This nineteenth-century invention,

this art of the mechanical age,
this beautiful language of light and movement, of myths and
adventure,
that can speak of love and hate,
of war and peace,
of life and death.
What would become of it?
And all these craftsmen, behind the cameras, behind the
lights, at the editing tables, would they have to unlearn
everything?
Would there ever be an electronic craft, a digital
craftsman?
And would this new electronic language be capable of
showing the *Citizens of the Twentieth Century* like the still
camera of August Sander or the film camera of John
Cassavetes?

## 18

We spoke of craftsmanship and of a craftsman's morals:
to build the true chair,
to design the true shirt,
in short, to find the essence of a thing in the process of
fabricating it.

## 19

In a different studio, with other collaborators, Yohji was
doing the fittings for his next Japanese collection, the
'domestic market'.
The atmosphere was different.
This time he was teaching. He was truly the master
surrounded by his students.

20

One day, we spoke of 'style' and how it might present an
enormous difficulty.
Style could become a prison,
a hall of mirrors in which you can only reflect and imitate
yourself.
Yohji knew this problem well.
Of course he had fallen into that trap. He had escaped from
it, he said, the moment he had learned to accept his own
style.
Suddenly the prison had opened up to a great freedom, he
said.
That, for me, is an author.
Someone who has something to say in the first place, who
then knows how to express himself with his own voice, and
who can finally find the strength in himself and the
insolence necessary to become the guardian of his prison
and not to stay its prisoner.


21

The photograph of Jean Paul Sartre that lay on the floor
was by Cartier-Bresson.
What interested Yohji was simply the collar: the collar on
the coat that Sartre wore.


21a

Not only clothes are fashionable,
buildings can be fashionable, too. Or cars, rock music
Swiss watches, books, movies . . .
Fashion can make things move.
Yohji was working on several collections simultaneously,
including his next one for men.
Was the approach different than for women?

*21b*

What was Yohji searching for in these old photographs?
Why did he surround himself with them even when they had no
direct connection to his work?


22

So, their mission was completed.
The show in Paris went well.
Immediately afterwards, the whole team had returned to the
studio to watch the tape of the show together.
This evening they would all go out and celebrate together.
Tomorrow they would all fly back to Tokyo together to begin
work the next day on the new collection.
It was only here, looking at these tired, but content faces
that I understood how Yohji's tender and delicate language
could survive in each of his creations:
these people, his assistants, his company which had
reminded me at times of a monastery, they were his
translators.
With all of their attentiveness, their care, their fervour,
they ensured that the integrity of Yohji's work remained
intact and they watched that the dignity of every dress,
every shirt, every jacket was preserved.
Inside an industrial production process, they were the
guardian angels of an author.


23

So I looked at them like they were a kind of film crew, and
Yohji among them was a director shooting a never-ending
film.
His images were not to be shown on a screen.
If you sat down to watch his film, you found yourself
instead in front of that very private screen which any

mirror that reflects your image can become.
To be able to look at your own reflection in such a way
that you can recognize and more readily accept your body,
your appearance, your history, in short, yourself,
that, it seems to me, is the continuing screenplay of the
friendly film by Yohji Yamamoto.


## 24

From the notebook of images that I collected over a certain
time as I was observing Yohji at work, I have saved my
favourite for last.
In a privileged moment, an electronic eye caught these
guardian angels on the job.

# The urban landscape from the point of view of images
(Delivered in English)

I am neither an architect nor a city planner. If I have any qualification to talk to you tonight about 'landscape from a point of view of images' as a film-maker, then it is because I am a traveller, because I have lived and worked in different cities in the world, because I have put up my camera in front of many landscapes, urban landscapes mostly, but also deserts. If this is qualification enough, is up to you to decide when you have listened to my little speech.

Anyway, I am honoured to have been invited here today. I am honoured by the fact that you, the specialists, are listening to me, an amateur. I thank the Delphi Research Company, the Steering Committee of the Architectural Design Conference 1991, and YKK for their trust and their kindness. I also want to apologize for the fact that I cannot possibly stay with you until tomorrow. For family reasons I absolutely have to be in Germany tomorrow, Sunday.

Let me start by saying that there are links between the cities, the urban landscapes and the cinema. Film is a city art. It has come into existence and it has blossomed together with the great cities of the world, since the end of the nineteenth century. Movies have witnessed their development from the quiet places they were at the turn of the century to the bursting and hectic megacities of today. Movies have witnessed their destruction during the wars, they have seen the skyscrapers go up, they have seen the ghettos, they have seen the rich get richer and the poor poorer. The cinema is the mirror of the twentieth-century city and twentieth-century mankind. Like no other art, films are the historic documents of our time. The seventh art, as it is called, is able to get to the essence of things, to capture the climate and the currents of their time, to express the hopes and the fears and the desires as a popular mass language like nothing else. Movies are also entertainment, and entertainment is the city's need par excellence. The cities just had to create cinema, cinema belongs in the city, and it reflects the city. It is this reflection that I want to talk about.

I have to make a new beginning. 'Urban landscape from the point of view of image.' I want you to consider the notion of 'image' for a moment. 'Image' is not such a clear-cut and stable definition. You all know how much the cityscapes have changed. You all know, for instance, how much Tokyo has changed in the last hundred, fifty, even ten years. These changes seem to happen faster and faster, and we have gotten used to the fact. But 'images' are also changing, in maybe a parallel development.

A long time ago, people made drawings on the walls of their caves. They carved into stones, or they drew into the sand. Later, they learned to paint. For a long time, painting was the only representation of reality. These paintings were unique, you had to be in front of the one existing canvas to see it. Then, with the invention of the printing press, images started to travel and to multiply, as etchings or drawings. The gigantic step forward, in the nineteenth century, was the invention of photography, and with that a whole new relation between reality and its representation. This was the beginning of 'second-hand reality'. The photographic images began to move, almost logically. For the first time, you could stay at home and see the world. Another thirty, forty years later, the photographic image had a competitor, the electronic image. It moved faster. It could show events 'live', without a delay. It was called television, which means 'seeing into the distance'. It did that, but it also created distance. It was colder, less emotional than the movies, and it took us further away from the idea that an image has a direct link with 'reality'. There was no more 'single' image, no negative like in the photographic process, and it needed a lot of technology to cross the distance from 'reality' to the viewer at home in front of the TV set. It also isolated people. You did not have to go out any more, stand in line and sit among strangers to enjoy a common, a social experience. And then television itself changed. There were more and more channels, and then there was cable, and satellites, and then there was video. You didn't have to rely on programming, you could do your own programming. And you couldn't see just preprogrammed tapes, you could also produce them yourself. The necessary technology became lighter and lighter, and cheaper and cheaper, and easier to handle. Now everybody can have a Handycam in their pocket. Every child can produce 'second-hand reality'. Of course, this is not the end. We are standing on the verge of the digital revolution and High-Vision. Electronic images have grown up. They are more beautiful and more detailed and more seductive than ever. They have also finally left behind the idea of the 'original'. Every copy is now identical to the original, every electronic image is available and reproducible almost everywhere in the world simultaneously. Electronic images are therefore more beautiful and more accessible than ever, *but* they are not necessarily more trustworthy. The digital image can be manipulated in every possible sense, and therefore can be falsified in every possible way. As there is no more original, there is also no more proof of 'Truth'. The digital electronic image has finally made the distance between 'reality' and 'second-hand reality' wider than ever. It has maybe even broken the link.

So, images have changed their nature completely. They have grown and multiplied at an unbelievable speed, and they continue to do so. We are bombarded with images like no other generation before. And this explosion will not stop; on the contrary, it will increase its acceleration. No authority, no institution, no government can prevent the further expansion of the visual realm. Computers, toys, gadgets, videophones, etc., are only adding to the inflation. People have learned to adapt themselves. They 'see faster', and they understand quicker. If you could present any contemporary action movie to an audience of the thirties, people would leave the theatre screaming with outrage or confusion. And if you put a TV-family of the fifties or sixties in front of a video screen today and let them zap through fifty channels, they would most likely fall into a stupor.

So, there are more and more images, they spread wider and wider, they invade our lives more and more, they are more beautiful *and* . . . they are more seductive. Films of the twenties and thirties (especially in Germany, but also in other parts of the world) had reinvented propaganda. The advertising industry, more than everybody else, learned from these seducing and convincing techniques. The new language of images that came with television changed the language of cinema, and then the new language of commercials changed both television *and* the cinema, so that today we are undoubtedly facing the fact that the spirit of advertising has sneaked into almost every area of visual communication. Images in general have become more 'commercial', they want our attention, they are in constant competition with each other, and each new one is trying to surpass the ones before. Images once had as a primary purpose to *show* something, that primary purpose is becoming more and more the tendency to *sell* something.

All this is abbreviated and, naturally, generalized. Why am I telling you this?

I think images have undergone a similar and parallel development to the one of our cities. Like them, our cities have grown out of proportion, and continue to do so. Like them, our cities have become colder, and more distanced. Like them, they are more and more alienated and alienating, like them they force us more and more to 'second-hand experiences', like them they become more and more commercially orientated. People have to move to the peripheries; the centres are too expensive. The centres are being taken over by business, hotels, entertainment. What's small, is disappearing. Only what is big can survive. Small and modest things disappear, just like small and modest images. In the movie industry that is a very obvious and sad loss. In the cities this is certainly even more obvious and certainly more severe.

And just as the imagery around becomes more cacophonic, disharmonic, loud and multifaceted, the cities become more and more complex, cacophonic, loud and overwhelming. They go well together. Our cities are bursting with images. Just look at the overflowing amount of images the cityscapes offer: the traffic signs, the huge neons on the roofs, the billboards and the posters, the shopfronts, the video walls, the newspaper stands, the vending machines, the messages painted on to cars and trucks, all the visual information inside every taxi or subway, there is something printed on to every plastic bag, etc. We are used to all that. When I first came to a city in the Eastern Bloc, it was Budapest, I went into a shock: there was nothing. A few traffic signs, some ugly banners, otherwise the city was empty of imagery, of advertising. That's when I realized how used I was to all that stuff, how addicted. Cities have become a drug, images are becoming drugs. Drugs carry the danger of overdose. What can we do to protect us?

In my business, or in my craft, or in my art, I found out that there was only one thing I was able to do to not let my images drown in the flood of all the others, and to not let them become the victims of the ongoing competitiveness and the overwhelming spirit of commercialization, and that was: to *tell a story*. In my business, craft or art, there is a danger that you want to produce images as a purpose in themselves. But I found out, that 'a beautiful image' is not of value in itself. On the contrary, a beautiful image can destroy the flow and the impact and the functioning of the whole, the dramatic structure. So I learned, from mistakes, that the only protection against the danger or the disease of the self-important image, was the belief in the priority of the story. I learned, that every image had a truth only in relation to the characters of that story. If the images took themselves too seriously, I found out, they diminished and weakened the characters. And with weakened characters, the story had no more energy. Only the story gave credibility to each image; it furnished a moral, so to speak, to my profession as an image-maker. So I ask myself, talking to people like you who create buildings and shape landscapes and structure our urban surroundings: is there a similar guidance? Can I continue with developing similarities between images and urban landscapes and try to find out if in your profession there is something as powerful as 'storytelling' is in mine?

I don't know. To get closer to an answer, I jump back. When I spoke about stories and how they can protect the characters of a film against self-indulgent and therefore superfluous or even harmful images, I realized that I somehow always think of the landscape in a scene as an additional character. A street, or a housefront, or a mountain, or a bridge, or a river or whatever are not just a 'background'. They also have a history, a 'personality', an identity that deserves to be taken seriously. They influence the human characters in the front of the frame, they create a mood, a sense of time, a certain emotion. They can be ugly or beautiful, old or young. But they are certainly 'present', and even for an actor that's all that counts. They deserve to be taken seriously. I worked in Australia over the last few years and I was fortunate to get to know the Aboriginal people a little bit. I was amazed to learn that for them every landscape formation embodies some figure from a mythical past. Every hill, every rock carries a 'story' that is related to their 'dreamtime'. And that reminded me, that as a child I had similar beliefs. A tree was not just a tree, but also a ghost, and the shapes of houses were like the shapes of faces. There were serious houses, and sinister houses, and friendly houses. A river could be frightening, but also soothing. Streets had personalities. There were some that I rather avoided and others that were good company. Mountains and shapes of the horizon were like definitions of certain longings or nostalgia, and I vividly remember my fear of a big rock in a forest that carried the name of 'sitting woman'. For a child, landscapes and cityscapes evoke emotions, associations, ideas, stories. We tend to forget that when we grow old. Basically, I think, we just learn to protect ourselves from the knowledge of our childhood, when we lived so much more out of our eyes, and when what we saw defined our sense of 'self' and of 'home'.

Talking about that rock, another rock comes to my mind. I lived in New York for a while, in an apartment facing Central Park. When I walked out of the building I faced a big black piece of rock that stood there just at the edge of the park. It had different colours depending on the weather. It was the sort of granite rock that the whole city was built on. And each time I looked at it, it gave me a feeling of orientation. It was so much older than the whole city around. It was solid. In a strange way it gave me confidence because I felt connected. I remember that I once smiled at it, as if it was a friend. It gave me some form of rest, it made me calmer. The city that I now live in is entirely built on sand, very white sand, and every now and then you can see a piece of it, even if it is only on a construction site. But that sand, too, gives me a feeling of connectedness, even of security. It tells me where I am. Of course, the buildings do that, too, but in a different way.

Berlin is a very peculiar city because it was so terribly damaged during the war, and because this destruction even continued afterwards through its dividedness. Berlin has a lot of empty spaces. You see houses that are completely blank on one side, because the neighbouring house was destroyed and is still missing. These bleak walls are called *Brandmauern* ('fire-walls') and you don't see them much in other cities. These empty spaces feel like wounds, and I like the city for its wounds. They show its history better than any history book or document. When I shot *Wings of Desire* I realized I was always looking for these empty spaces, these no-man's-lands. I felt the city defined itself much better where it was empty than where it was full.

If there is too much to see, that is, if an image is too full, or if there are too many images, the effect is: you don't see anything any more. Too much turns quickly into 'nothing'. You all know that. You also know the other effect: if an image is empty, or almost empty, and sparse, it can reveal so much that it completely fills you, and the emptiness becomes 'everything'. As a film-maker, you face that problem every time you try to set up a shot. Just as much as you want to frame something in order to show it, you have to be aware of keeping things out of your frame. What you want to show, what you want *in*, is defined by what you keep *out*.

But to come back to the empty spaces. I have a strong feeling in Berlin, where I live, that the empty spaces allow the visitor and the people of Berlin to see through the cityscape. Not only in the sense that they can see through the *space*, and even see the horizon, which anyway is a pleasant experience in a city, but they can also see through these gaps in a sense that they can see through *time*. In life, time defines history. In a movie you can experience something similar. Some films are like closed walls: there is not a single gap between its images that would allow you to see anything else than what this movie shows you. Your eyes and your mind are not allowed to wander. You cannot *add* anything from yourself to that particular film, no feelings, no experience. You stumble out empty afterwards, like you have been abused. Only those films with gaps in between their imagery are telling stories, that is my conviction. A story only exists and comes to life in the mind of the viewer or listener. Those other films, the closed systems, only pretend to tell stories. They use the recipes for storytelling, but all their ingredients have no taste.

Cities do not tell stories. But they can tell *history*. Cities can show and carry their history; they can make it visible, or they can hide it. They can open your eyes, like movies, or they can close them. They can leave you abused, or they can nourish your imagination.

Tokyo, unlike what many people seem to think of it, is an open city for me, a city that not only steals but gives. Of course, it has its side of overload, of constant assault. But in the most amazing ways you can also just turn around the corner, and you step into a clearing. Out of the noisiest jungle you can all of a sudden enter into a quiet, tender, restful area. Next to skyscrapers you find alleyways of little houses, with gardens, birds, cats, peace. Or you find a cemetery, and unlike cemeteries in America or Europe, these are inhabited, lively places. Or you find a temple, and unlike the churches we know, you can centre yourself, you don't feel like you are intruding if you are not religious. Tokyo is a system of islands.

Of course, these islands have to be preserved; but of course you see them disappear. As I said before: everything that is small disappears. But if we lose everything that is small, we lose our direction, we become the victims of the *big*, the unpenetrable, the overpowering. We have to fight for everything small that is left. The small puts the big into a perspective. In the history of cinema the small films were the cradle of creativity, of new ideas, of daring messages, of human and warm and true stories. The small movies were the think-tanks. In a city, the small, the empty, the open are the batteries that allow us to recharge, that protect us against the assault of the big.

I am not against big buildings. On the contrary, I like them, I love the monoliths, the skyscrapers. But at the same time, I only think they are bearable and livable with, if you can step out and find the alternative, the alleyway with a small shop and a small café. No other city offers both at the same time like Tokyo.

When 'Les Halles', the cast-iron market halls of Paris were torn down, I stood there, weeping with fury. For years there was nothing but a big hole. Now there is a gigantic system of underground shops and boutiques, that for me still has the face of the big hole. When the Golden Gai in Shinjuku is torn down to make room for some big structure, I will cry, too, and Tokyo will be poorer.

Don't misunderstand me. I am not against building new houses, restructuring the face of a city. That would mean being opposed to film-making, with the argument that every new film would only add to the inflation of images. No, refusal cannot be the solution. Every building in itself can stand as an example and can express ideas of clarity and simplicity, can serve as a new standard of function and aesthetic value. But you, the architects, have to face the fact that it will appear in a context that might drown it, just as I as a film-maker have to face the fact that my film might play in a multiplex cinema together with films of violence, or pornos or whatever. My film might end up on television, and people might zap through it on their search through fifty channels. So I have to hope that each shot, or at least each scene, expresses a serenity and a gentleness that would create the difference between it and a merely commercial product. By that, I don't mean to enter the competition and the vicious circle of images competing for attention. I rather mean to step out of this contest. You can only set an example by trying to be true to yourself, not by trying to follow the trend. You have to be the author of the building and see it through from the first sketch to the moment it is inhabited, just like a film-maker has to control and shape their movie from the first treatment to the moment it is shown to the audience. A building and a film have much in common. They have to be planned, designed and financed. You have to have a solid structure that supports it, like a story carries a film. You have to give it its own definite style, just like a film needs its own coherent language. You have to make it transparent and inhabitable. A film, too, needs to be lived in, lived with.

So, to end my speech, I am asking you to look at your work for a moment as the task of creating biographical background for future children, with city- and landscapes that will furnish their imaginations with images. And I also want you to consider the opposite of what you do by definition – not only to construct buildings, but to create open space to preserve emptiness, so we are not only faced with *fullness*, but have the emptiness in which to repose.

## Find myself a city to live in
Conversation with Hans Kollhoff

HANS KOLLHOFF: *Are you surprised to have architects coming to you for your views on architectonics or city planning?*

WIM WENDERS: 'Architectonics' would surprise me, 'city planning' less so, because that's something I'm interested in. I think that comes through in my films, because I think films are a part of city life, like music or paintings, and architects who are interested in city planning ought to know something about paintings and music and cinema. How else are they going to be able to talk about cities and the people who live in them?

*I came to the conclusion that film-makers and architects don't just face a lot of the same problems, but that film-makers are actually thinking about certain issues a lot harder, more precisely and rather quicker, things that only dawned on architects and urban planners a lot later, if at all. For instance, here you are, talking about the system of film-distribution: 'That brutality marks a film from its making right through to its distribution, and this loveless dealing with images is killing our language. You can understand perhaps how an industry finds it impossible to be idealistic, but its contempt for its products and its customers is beyond belief. That needs to change.' And in the same context, talking about* The American Friend, *you say it doesn't have any explicit political content, but it doesn't patronize its audience, it doesn't make its characters into puppets, nor its audience either, and what was at issue was popular cinema. I thought a parallel might be drawn here with 'popular architecture', to coin a phrase, and that would be very much to the point.*

Yes, that's true, let's think about that. I need to make a mental leap.

*Do you mean a jump in time?*

No, mainly from the idea of talking about films that have something to do with architecture, to talking about architecture directly. The main connection, it seems to me, is that both are art-forms that have a lot to do with money, and are still concerned with the question that most preoccupies people, namely: 'How should we live?' The cinema has a different sort of answer than architecture. The way architecture asks the question is of course much more 'concrete' and long-term. People actually live inside what's built, a film just asks the question and might occasionally answer it one way or another – whereas architecture is always question and answer at once, and maybe the answer is 'for keeps, for the rest of your life'. That, thank God, isn't the case with cinema, you can walk out of a film if you want to. People can't turn their backs on a building in quite the same way. And a city – once it's been redesigned in one way or another, there might be hundreds of thousands of people who are stuck in it. So you live with architecture differently than you do with a film, but even so, both ask the same question: 'How should we live?' Before you make a film and before you change a city, you ask the same question. The entertainment industry never asks that question. I remember saying once that there is no such thing as an unpolitical film; all films, especially entertainment films, are political. The less a film has to say about politics, the more political it probably is. The less architecture asks itself at the outset, 'How should we live?', the more it suppresses the question, the more someone will probably have to suffer for it later on. So what is entertainment architecture, if it's analogous to the entertainment industry? It's what you build with the intention of meeting the smallest opposition and the most favour, i.e. as big a sale and as big a profit as possible. In cinema, that's an entertainment film. Always with the excuse, 'It's what people want, isn't it?' I would think that entertainment architecture models itself on Hollywood.

*The cheapest and easiest way to cause as much euphoria as possible . . .*

. . . that's right, and the kind of euphoria that comes from publicity and promises. You may find yourself being entertained – it does happen – but as you leave you generally feel amazed at what you've had to put up with for it. You come out, and you feel empty and drained; it's like you haven't been given anything, only paid two hours of your time for a noisy roaring in your ears, and nothing's changed. The film sucked up to me, and I endured it for a couple of hours. Maybe entertainment architecture's like that too, because it charms the pants off you, and only when you're living in it do you notice you're the one who's paying for it and not the other way round – you're not getting anything from it, only giving.

*Let's try and be a bit more specific. Another point, another possible parallel seems to me what you do with the past, and in that respect it seems that cinema and architecture are out of step. As I'm sure you know, we're currently in a phase of rampant eclecticism, not only architecturally but also in urban planning – returning to old squares, old city borders, etc. – which also gave architects certain grounds for hope, the hope of finding some continuity, not only in basic urban patterns, but also with the traditions of architecture, having something to go back to or picking up the thread wherever it broke. But then it very soon became apparent that people weren't using history properly – as a living tradition – but only as a source of authority or legitimacy for whatever they were doing anyway, using ostensibly 'traditional' ideas as an alibi. It was just a cover for themselves, not to develop anything living.*

In film there are two ways of using the past. There are films that are based on 'classical models', and that offer those models as a kind of alibi. In the 1970s in Germany there was a spate of films based on famous novels, mostly from the nineteenth century. It was symptomatic of a lack of interest in stories of 'today'. And it is a problem for the Germans, because they've learned not to trust their own stories. The Americans are better off, they're the other way, they have blind faith in their stories. So much so that Hollywood now does nothing but keep on rehashing those same old stories. The American cinema today is feeding almost entirely off itself, dealing in experiences that only come out of other films. The connection between films and life, the notion that films deal with 'true-life experiences', is gone. Maybe there is a parallel there with architecture, if architects have stopped asking themselves 'How do people want to live?' and only ask 'How have successful buildings been made lately?'

*You have an eye for urban planning. I'm thinking of a scene in* Wings of Desire, *in Friedrichstadt\*, where the circus was situated. The southern*

---

\*Area of former East Berlin around the Friedrichstrasse (Trans.).

*part of the Friedrichstadt is one of those places which has changed*
*enormously over the past five years, all because of planners coming along*
*appealing to tradition. It must have been difficult, while filming, to isolate*
*it as a location, because of the new old world springing up behind it . . .*

I chose the place because of its isolation, because it was a unique kind of
place that brought all kinds of different things together, and there were all
these changes underway. It's right at the bottom end of the Friedrichstrasse, where it turns into that square . . .

*The Belle-Alliance-Platz as was, now the Mehringplatz . . .*

Just north of that square is an enormous no-man's-land criss-crossed by
actual trails, and if you stand in the middle of it where the circus used to
be, you have completely different views in four directions, views of the
past, or of relics of the past, witnesses of the past. On one side there's that
typical Berlin thing that you hardly ever find in other cities, one of those
gigantic 'firewalls' of sheer brick that lines the whole square to the north.
On the south side there's that really hideous view of a three-storey car
park with an apartment block behind it. It's not just a film for Berliners, I
want Berlin to represent the whole world, and I thought someone, say,
living in New York won't ever have seen one of those huge blank brick
walls. In Paris, there are hardly any buildings where you can see the
sidewalls like that. Those walls are like history books, if you like. They tell
you all about loss and defeat in history. Unfortunately, now they're
starting to be plastered over, with official approval too, and that makes
them 'unreadable'.

We spent literally weeks combing the city looking for the place to set up
our circus, and that was the emptiest site I saw. It seemed like the still
centre of a centrifuge, the eye of the hurricane of the city. In that place
there was suddenly a great sense of peace, there were mice and rabbits,
and we could let our elephant trample around there. There were children
playing, and you could see the city around you on all sides, like an open
history book. It had something exemplary about it. There was even that
one house on the corner of the Wilhelmstrasse that was built around a
courtyard, like a medieval fortress. One corner has been taken out of it,
and through it you could see into the yard; there was an enormous tree

growing in it that you wouldn't have known was there from the outside. Finding it was like a dream, and I thought, a place like that won't exist for much longer. That's why we filmed there. In all my films I've looked for locations that might disappear before too long.

Another scene comes to mind, on the Langenscheidt Bridge: a couple of months later, that was gone. For me it was far and away the most attractive bridge in the whole city, and I don't know why it had to go. They'll put up a new bridge in its place, but it won't cross anything. You'll just drive over it without even realizing it's a bridge. The way bridges are now. On old bridges you always had the feeling you were crossing over something. That bridge used to be the way into Kreuzberg. I'm not strictly speaking a true Berliner, I've not lived here for 20 or 30 years, but I could feel it clearly: that bridge has a history, and it's enriched the lives of all those people who crossed it every day of their lives. It really hurt when it went. And then they went and left one of its supports standing! One of its arches is still up, not supporting anything, just standing there like a witness to its destruction. Maybe that's 'entertainment architecture' or 'entertainment urban planning': you leave a bit of the past as 'entertainment', or maybe because you feel guilty for having demolished something, so you leave one of its supports standing to appease your guilt. I really think it would be better to demolish the whole thing and have done with it. A support like that just serves to demonstrate the guilty consciences of those people who demolished the rest.

*But can you imagine a new bridge being built that doesn't just replace the function of the old one, but that has something of its quality, though in a quite different style? Or don't you think that's possible?*

No, I do, I think the sort of bridge you describe is perfectly possible, only the one they're putting up now isn't one. I think it's possible even today to build bridges that provide an experience, on which you notice this is like a ford, through the city, and now you're going from one part of it to another. It is possible, but then you can't just put down some concrete thing where you no longer have any sense of something being 'bridged'. A bridge should be a place that makes you ponder, and feel the act of crossing!

*You once said you wouldn't care to make a film that couldn't have cars in it, or TV aerials or television wires.*

Yes, but it's not because I'm so smitten with TV aerials, but because I once made a historical film, and I noticed I wasn't interested in filming in a place that wasn't lived in or real, but was artificially created, and where things like aerials and phone lines had to be hidden away out of sight.

*What I'm trying to get at is really this: there is a documentary quality about it when you say, Will you look at this car park and these firewalls, and in the case of the firewalls it may well be that they won't be around much longer. But leaving that aside, and here is the problem that we architects are facing too, there is another quality that isn't just documentary, but that's more like fiction. So my question is this: where is the dividing line, where do things like a car or a garage begin to become part of the urban scene, or, put it another way, can you imagine those things as having their own expressive possibilities? I know they do in America.*

Yes, absolutely, the mythology of American cities in movies is proof of that. But you don't have to bring in America. European cities have different myths of their own.

*So my question then: what happens when you memorialize things, when you look out for authentic images, what is the relationship between documentary and fiction? Maybe using the same example, of the Friedrichstadt.*

In films, the fiction, the story, is like the First Cause. Without it, sure, I could make documentaries, but I'm not really interested in that, I want to tell a story. The fiction gives me somewhere to be, it's what allows me to set up my camera at all. In this instance, it's the story of the angel and the trapeze artist. And this story, which I'm getting 5 million marks to make a film of, on its own, I think, is completely empty and cold and lacking in reality, unless it manages, in the course of telling itself, to latch onto something. If it doesn't succeed in finding something 'real', then it'll remain fiction from beginning to end, and fiction on its own in the cinema is a waste. Pure fiction is like a cartoon film, where you don't see anything of the real world. It has a tendency to make you shut your eyes to the world, to make you forget about the world. And film, as the pre-eminent art-form of the twentieth century, I would say, should be reminding you about the world, not helping you to escape it. Of course, an entertainment film would like nothing better than to make you forget about the world. Entertainment means distraction from reality. But I think films were invented not to distract people from the world, but to point them back at it. Obviously that implies a certain conflict with fiction, because the fiction is trying to point at something different. But at the same time, films that are really serious about telling their stories strike me as being the only 'genuine' documentaries. For example, when I look at Alfred Hitchcock's *Vertigo*, which he made in San Francisco in the early 1960s – and I lived there a year myself – then what I knew about the city then and what I still know about it now is powerfully influenced by that film. Of course, even though the film – like all of Hitchcock – is pure fiction, the city it was filmed in is a powerful presence that finally forms a large part of what sticks in your mind about the film. In that way, I think that every film that really grabs you by its story can also grab you as documentary.

*You said you thought film was the art-form for our century . . .*

Yes, because unlike theatre or painting or literature, it actually moves in our space, in and out of our cities, or from country to country. It moves about in our world.

*If you look at films from the 1920s that are to do with cities, and compare them to* Wings of Desire, *for example, the cities were always characterized by the amount of activity, noise, bustle, flux; of course, that has something to do with people's euphoria about big-city life in those days, whereas we've become rather disillusioned.*

Yes, but there were always films around too that didn't see cities as something euphoric or galvanizing; there are films where the cities are oppressive, and where the individual man or woman is completely adrift. There are those sort of films too, especially in the 1920s and 30s.

*Anyway, that was something that struck me, and* Wings of Desire, *in*

*those scenes that had a strong effect on me, in the Friedrichstrasse for*
*instance, is completely the opposite. What you experience in them is*
*emptiness and a kind of tranquillity. Of course, the view of a place is*
*predicated on a certain distance. The camera didn't dive into the mêlée,*
*and I was wondering if that's a true image of a big city today, in the late*
*twentieth century?*

Unfortunately not. I only wish that other cities had as many backwaters
or 'blind spots' as Berlin. It is really extraordinary that a city like Berlin
has all this empty space everywhere. There are so many of those sites,
places like on the Friedrichstrasse, or the Potsdamer Platz, which is in the
film too. In other cities like New York or Tokyo or Paris or London – no,
London has a bit of that sort of thing too, but not in the centre, more in
the outskirts – you never suddenly find yourself with a clear sight of the
horizon, across an empty wasteland full of scrub and weeds. I think it's
one of the most extraordinary things about Berlin, the fact that those
wildernesses still exist.

*You're talking about the sort of places you'd tend to find more on the*
*periphery of other cities.*

Yes, and you can't really even say what they do. They don't have a
function, and that's the great thing about them. The Potsdamer Platz was
amazing the way it was, now they've planted lawns everywhere, prettified
it up, and it's nothing, it doesn't exist any more. It used to be a kind of
wilderness. And I guess it's impossible to get that across to someone in
planning terms, some sort of committee, that the best thing about their
city are those places that nobody's done anything about. I guess a city by
definition is going to *want* to do something with those spaces. It's a
tragedy. That area off the Friedrichstrasse is one of the most beautiful
places in Berlin, right after the Potsdamer Platz. Spaces like that can't last,
they're completely anachronistic, they've not been the subject of any
purposeful planning, and in the long run no self-respecting city can have
places in it that aren't subject to plans and whatever. It reminds me of
Brasilia, which I visited once, because it fascinated me, the idea of a city
that was totally planned. I went for walks a lot there, although it's not
easy to walk there – the place didn't really allow for that. You need to

walk for miles because of the stupid planning . All the hotels in the city are in one block, so you have all the hotels together, and none at all anywhere else. It's a kind of 1950s euphoria you get there, and the incredible thing is that although everything had been planned to the *n*th degree, there was 'life' in the place in spite of it: they had a kind of flea market on a big open space that was meant to be a park, and a kind of invasion took place of people who needed disorder in their deadly planned city. That unplanned spot was the best and the only living place in the city. And I think Berlin has an extraordinary number of these spontaneously created places. For me, a city's 'quality of life' is directly related to whatever 'neglect' it permits.

*That's rather a depressing thing for architects to hear.*

Yes, but they could learn a lot from it.

*Let's go back to the original question, what brings you back to Berlin. After so much time abroad, in New York and in Tokyo, why Berlin? In a sense I'm in the same position as you, because I was in the States myself for some time before coming back here. And if you look at Germany from a distance, Berlin is really the only place where you can imagine working, because the feeling and the life here has so much of that electricity that you only get in a modern city.*

Sure. Well, first thing, I need to be in a city. And especially coming from America, where there are cities that are really out on a limb. Some of them I really really like, like San Francisco and Houston and New York. There I have everything around me that I need, in terms of material things and vibes too. But at the same time you're conscious of missing something too, if you're in America, that isn't anything to do with the layout of the cities or anything. So you go back to Europe, or back to Germany, and there really isn't a lot of choice. You miss something there too. Munich's a bit small and provincial and rootsy and museum-ish, and Hamburg is cold and snotty, and Düsseldorf is terribly nouveau and pleased with itself, and Frankfurt's such a disaster that really the only place that seems at all possible is Berlin. If you've been away a long time, you feel differently about Germany. I think I only became German by living abroad for seven years. And that thing, 'being German', is nothing as grand as 'history' or 'sense of patriotism'. It's more to do with faces and gestures or things people say sitting opposite you on the subway, things you can hardly put your finger on, tiny things really. Maybe from childhood – the environment you grew into as a child, which you can't really describe either. And that is made up of things like different kinds of houses and doors and windows than you get elsewhere, different cars and different street-lamps. And in Berlin, I think it really is the way I was hoping Germany would be when I was in the States. In a lot of West German cities, I can imagine being blindfolded and taken to a place and having the blindfold taken off and being asked: 'So where is this?' and I'd need to see an advertising hoarding or a street sign or something to know I was in Germany, and not in Kansas City or Zurich or Singapore. In Berlin you always know you're in Berlin. And that's an important thing for a city, to be unmistakeable.

I once lived in Frankfurt for a year, and it's as though that year had disappeared from my life. I didn't acquire any new habits, didn't have any favourite walks or haunts, no favourite anything. No attachment, not even to 'applewine', nothing. At most, the central railway station; I was forever going in and out of there, and so the Haupbahnhof became my spiritual home, not my apartment or my street or the whole city. But then you leave the station, and it's gone. Berlin doesn't have anywhere like the Frankfurt Hauptbahnhof. The only place in Berlin that's at all like that is the Staatsbibliothek, and maybe the museums, yes, the museums in East and West Berlin. That's something you shouldn't forget either, the thing that makes Berlin unique in the world, namely that you've always got the other side of it too. Normally you'd have to go from New York, say, to Chicago, whereas here the nearest city is just a block away. Getting from West to East Berlin, you make the kind of journey that might otherwise involve a flight or a long drive, whereas here it's just five minutes on the S-Bahn. I think that's quite weird. Each time I go there, I'm amazed; I just can't get used to the idea of such a short ride taking you into a different world. I get annoyed with myself for not using the opportunity more often than I do. When I'm in East Berlin, I think it has to be laziness or stupidity or something that stops people from going more often. I know loads of people in West Berlin who haven't been at all. Somehow it's a drag to get to, or they shrug their shoulders and say, oh yeah, East Berlin. It's mind-boggling to think it used to be one city. Imagine what it was like in the 1920s or 30s! It must have been incredibly big. And I like that a lot about Berlin too, that you're forever being reminded of the past, and not sort of between quotation marks, but as a really living sensation. That's what makes Berlin such a creative city for me. It's a city that gives you energy for your work. I can speak with a bit of authority on this; there are a lot of cities I've had to leave because I just never did anything while I was there. I spent four years in L.A., and never did a thing. Nor in San Francisco or Paris. There are cities where you just never get anything done. You get there, and somehow you get the sense on your first day in a place, that this is just another one of those cities that will just drain you, and it'll end up really costing you being there. I think Berlin's the opposite. In Berlin, I think you keep getting given things.

*It seems to me the opening sequences of* Wings of Desire, *with the radio-mast and the ICC and the firewalls, is pretty much the antithesis of what you get in contemporary urban planning and whatever planners or lay-people think of as a working city. And that in turn reminded me of a picture in your Tokyo book of those walls with the huge billboards on them, and trains whizzing by in the foreground. I'd like to go back to the subject of the city in the twentieth century, if I may. In the Tokyo book you admitted on the one hand that you were sad at no longer finding Ozu's sort of imagery around, but on the other hand that you found yourself strongly attracted by the concentration of it and the breaches with traditional form and style – and those are feelings that I share – but I wonder how that can be translated or imported. We'd need to have a totally different spatial sense, a different notion of order, a different scale of priorities, but I wonder if we can draw from that creativity, instead of always destroying things in order to build order.*

Well, when I think of Tokyo, I don't suppose there's any greater planning disaster anywhere in the world than Tokyo. Nothing there is planned. There's no style and no idiom and nothing is managed, and it's just utter chaos. It looks as though it slid from the Middle Ages into the year 2000, without any guiding hand whatever. There are factories dotted about all over the city, and people living round them, you aren't aware of any separation into districts or zones. Everything is mixed, there are no separate districts for rich and poor. The poor seem to live all round, and the rich are in the middle of it too. There are skyscrapers everywhere, and pressed up against them some little hovels, and then you have a bank or something – everything's a complete muddle. At the same time, when I think of Tokyo, I get really homesick. There is something that gives the people that live there a real quality of life, in all that bustle. For all the unbelievable chaos, for instance, I always got to every appointment on time, whether I went by subway or taxi.

*It might be the sheer number of possibilities that make a city like that; you know, you go out of your front door and something unexpected happens to you. In terms of the number of permutations possible, maybe you could compare Berlin and Tokyo. Both of them equally chaotic. Have you heard of August Endell? He was a painter and an architect. In the 20s he wrote a little book about Berlin called* The Beauty of the Big City.

Afraid I don't . . .

*It's a very atmospheric description of the city in the 1920s, the same city you see in the films of the period, but not many people ever managed to put it into words. Well, he has this idea of 'Heimat', of a spiritual home, and he makes it clear that it's the layering of experience that makes a place 'home'. It reminded me of you. He says home has to be made, and is only created in the eye of a person who's looking for it. And he says something that we might go back to in a moment, namely that buildings and cities, though they might look bleak and lifeless and intimidating for the moment, actually have a completely different kind of beauty, like a kind of industrial beauty, and he goes on to talk about machinery and mechanical movement. Endell says there are basically two possibilities, either to change the way we build our cities, which is a very far-reaching kind of project, or else make up for their deficiencies by looking at them in a different kind of way. Become aware of a type of beauty in them that we hadn't considered . . .*

It sometimes occurs to me too that it might be preferable to generate a different type of response, rather than turn to a different type of planning. If you think of whatever old images of cities you have, whether it's *Metropolis* or New York or Berlin in the 1920s, I think you can say there's a type of beauty you only find in cities; it doesn't correspond to any conventional objective ideas of beauty, but still gives you a kind of lift. I mean you can't really say the New York subway is a thing of beauty, but you can enjoy it. Or think of traffic. There's a way of getting along in a city, or with a city, climbing into the flow of it, which is quite exhilarating. And then you might find that 'planning measures' actually inhibit that or kill it. To me the idea of streets where there's all kinds of stuff going on, cars hooting and switching lanes and running the lights, is just more appealing than a pedestrian precinct. That's what's really urban. And I'd sooner be in the flow of the city, than be dragooned in some way. I think it's really important for people who live in a city to be allowed to get on with it. Whereas to deny that or cover it over, to pedestrianize it, that just . . .

*Puts you in mind of a village . . .*

Cuts off your contact with the city. You're dealt this fake kind of beauty and fake functionalism. Can you imagine how ghastly the Ku'damm would be with no cars on it? Thank God it's too big for that. But think of all the streets it did happen to! The fascinating thing about cities is how you adjust to them, all the cars and whatnot. Those wonderful double-decker buses here in Berlin. I'm sorry the trams have gone, but they still have those in the East. Then again, you have the U-Bahn and the S-Bahn. That's one of Berlin's great assets as a city, all the different ways of getting around. In Los Angeles, there isn't anything at all, you simply have to have a car. Or you get yourself a bicycle, which is what I ended up doing in New York, and I got around faster than if I'd been taking taxis or even the subway. That is a great feeling. It puts you even more in touch with the city. It's really exhilarating, being on a bike, and getting into an enormous traffic system; it's like you're part of a great migration or something. You feel more cut off in a car, whereas I love public transport in cities, or walking along at a tremendous pace. It takes crowds and bustle for me to really feel at home in a city. All this is really just to say that there is something in cities that you just have to experience for yourself, which can be beautiful, and which it's a mistake for planners to try and eliminate.

*It sounds to me more like the kind of thing you miss when you haven't got it, than what you actually enjoy at the time.*

Yes, you could be right. You can get so wrapped up in a city that you only feel its advantages when you're missing them.

*I wonder whether your kind of eye – which finds beauty in firewalls, and those sort of lines and contours – whether that isn't the kind of detached perspective of someone who isn't essentially involved with those things. But maybe not, because I can imagine that children, in particular, might pick up on and remember things that the rest of us are supposed to find crummy.*

Oh, I'm sure those bare brick walls live longer in the memory than any painted façades. And yes, 'crummy' or decrepit things are better at digging themselves into the memory than intact things. If you think about it, the beat-up things have a rough surface that memory grips onto, while it slips off the slicker surface of things that are neat and new and pristine. I suppose you can also measure a city by what it gives to the memory, and there are places that give nothing at all, that don't have anything at all that sticks in the mind. In Berlin, you find things worthy of remembering all over. It's possible that faintly down-at-heel things stick in the mind more. When I remember Glasgow, I remember the bits that were pretty decayed, and I have no memory of the centre, which looked just like any other place. I can picture other cities too that time has got to work on. That's an important factor as well, that you can see the work of time. In Berlin, you can see that all over the place. It's only in the new suburbs that you find yourself catapulted out of time, into a kind of historically neutral environment. A big city can give you an unrivalled sense of time. I find there's always a terrific leap when I go from Berlin to Paris. I'm living in both places at once right now, because my girl-friend lives in Paris, so some of the time we're in Berlin and the rest of it in Paris. It's just as good a place to live in as Berlin, but you're in a completely different element just by virtue of the fact that just about everything's intact. Virtually every street is a complete row of buildings, and there are loads and loads of streets and buildings from the last century or earlier, which gives you the sense of being in a closed and intact environment with an unbroken surface. Berlin's the opposite, there's nothing unbroken about Berlin. You're forever being thrown from one impression to the next, which is completely different. In Berlin, you have to piece together the history from all the fragments. Paris gives you the feeling of being in an unbroken narrative.

*Except for the suburbs.*

Sure. But I meant in the actual city. Even if you come out of a side-street onto the Champs Elyśees or one of the grands boulevards, you have continuity. But in Berlin, if you come out of a side-street onto, say, the Bismarckstrasse, you go from one era to another, and that's happening the whole time. There's something about that that creates energy, and so I get a terrific buzz from Berlin, because there are always things facing each other that don't belong there, so it gets like walking around between a pair of magnets.

*Another of the things we architects suffer from is the fact that we're never offered anything entire – though cities weren't built in that way either. Plans are forever being drawn up, but only a tiny percentage of them were ever carried out, there was never an overall concept for the city. Berlin never had anything like that. People kept offering some overall blueprint, but really they could be pretty sure they'd only get to make a small fraction of it. There's something ambivalent about that, I find. On the one hand, we suffer on account of it, on the other it produces that tension and electricity you were describing.*

Berlin is an utterly contemporary city. If you think of these two cities [East and West Berlin] in one that no longer exists, I think there's something really contemporary about that set-up, really in tune with 1988 and what's going on in the world, and what people are thinking about. Berlin keeps you on your toes because it's not a closed system the way most other cities are, it keeps giving you a jolt. And that's really what I look to a city for, for it to keep giving my ideas a shaking. All types of planning, by definition, are attempts to impose some kind of homogeneity, whereas for me a 'city' means the opposite of that. A city has to embrace contradictions, a city should be an explosive kind of a place.

*You have a similar problem in films, don't you? A film, as I understand it, aspires to some kind of unity, but it also tends to want to burst at the seams.*

Yes, agreed. Just like every other kind of expression, a painting or poem or whatever. Everything aspires to that closed form, but excitement only happens when it breaks out, when something slips out of control. If everything is seamlessly whole, there's no room to experience anything. That's as true of films as anything else.

*Although perhaps unity is more easily achievable, so you need to be more wary of it. Isn't that why you put 'to be continued' at the end, as a way of saying, this isn't unity?*

I put that because it seemed odd to me to have made a film that's just getting going as it ends. Also because, while I'd run out of time and money, I really wanted to go on with the story. At any rate, I'd reached a point where a new story might begin, so I put 'to be continued'. If you imagine that, as it were, up in the sky, like sky-writing, 'to be continued', there are cities where you couldn't possibly put that, because they don't offer any possible sequel. But having it in *Wings of Desire** actually emblazoned in the sky over Berlin, that seemed really appropriate to me. Berlin is a city that cries out for a sequel. Even though there are these ties with the past everywhere, Berlin is also a city where you keep on stubbing your toe on the future. At this point I'm really just thinking aloud, but isn't there a way in which cities have to negotiate between past and future; either they make the future accessible to you, or they get in the way of it. I think cities have that kind of role. They create a sense of time for their inhabitants in that no-man's-land between the past and the future. There are cities that spur you on to change, and I think Berlin's one of them. I'm not being political when I say that, I'm just talking about change as a general ethos, or environment. And that's why there are so many cities in West Germany that are like dead ends, that are absolutely perspectiveless. When I think of my hometown of Düsseldorf, everything in it has been so styled to a kind of perfection that it has to stay exactly as it is. It's been gussied up to the last paving stone, and they might as well start charging

*Original title: *The Sky over Berlin* – Trans.

admission: Düsseldorf Museum, as it were. Munich is the most fixed city in the world as far as I'm concerned. It's difficult to talk about cities, because they can be expressed in images much more readily than in words. That's why I like American thrillers so much, from Hammett to Chandler to Ross Macdonald. Those are all writers who are good on cities. There aren't any cities in literature to match Hammett's San Francisco or Chandler's Santa Monica. Writing about cities is a rare art, they're such elusive places. Too much of them needs to be experienced: they need to be smelled and heard and used and seen – above all, they need to be seen.

There was a point in our conversation, by the way, that I wanted to expand on, when we were talking about historical films. The wretched thing about historical films, especially when they're set in cities, is when you notice, oh yes, they've certainly done a lot of tidying up here, they've taken down all the TV aerials, and cleaned everything up. I've never yet seen a historical film that had a dirty car drive right through a shot. Everything is always frantically clean, and even if you have a street in New York, say, at the turn of the century, you'll notice that even the rubbish is clean. It's an idea of history that edits everything out. The thing I wanted to add was that I often got that sort of feeling in cities, where they've tried to do up something old. I get the feeling I'm in a historical film. You just know it never looked like that, not even when it was brand new. It's not a way of evoking or being faithful to the past, it's turning the past into a cliché version of itself. That happened lately in Berlin, East and West, when both cities got into a cleanliness contest for the 500th anniversary of Berlin; lots of places were so dolled up, you couldn't see the history any more, only that cliché version of history. Renovating is a bit of a tightrope walk anyway, a bit too clean, or too much façade, and you might as well be in Disneyland. It's a difficult thing to put something new next to something old. But at the same time, I think that's the most exciting thing you can do in a city, that juxtaposition of the old and the new. I think that's incredibly exciting, but wherever the new thing tries to reach out to the old, or connect with it in some way, the results are almost invariably awful. It's easy to say that, but whether it's possible to plan it so that it comes off, I'm less sure about. I suppose you just try to make your new construction as good as it can be. At least that way the results are better than if you try and build bridges between the old and the new.

*Are there places in Berlin that you can think of, where something new has been put up next to something old, and complements it or enhances it?*

The obvious example would be the Gedächtniskirche. But that's too much of a monument, you can't really count that. I've always liked the Nationalgalerie with the Stüler church behind it. It always struck a chord with me, the new Nationalgalerie building, backed by that old church. But of course there are loads more examples here in Berlin. But there's even more in the States.

*In New York, classically.*

Yes, New York has some amazing examples of different eras juxtaposed.

*Yes, it's because of the way they deal with zoning and planning there. Within each separate zone, everyone can do pretty much as he pleases, and that's encouraged by the most daring regulations . . .*

. . . yes, they help, and I really like that about America, it gives this wonderful playfulness and risk to a lot of new buildings there. The whole of Houston looks to me as if a playful imagination had been at work, not doing anything concerted, but where everyone says to himself, I'm going to build something, let's say green and all glass. And the next guy comes along and builds something without a roof, just a leaning wall. Each building is like a haiku, and each one tries to stand out from the crowd. I like that a lot about Houston, which is a city that barely existed twenty years ago. It's quite rigorous, there's nothing compromising about it, and that makes it a statement of what's possible in architecture today. Whereas the whole skyline of Frankfurt hasn't a single building in it that asked the question: What is possible?, not one. Depressing. Look out the window, it's just one block after another! Not a trace of imagination anywhere, not one that wanted to show the others. I'm sure that isn't all you need to put up a good building, but at some point a kind of sporting ambition or individualism is surely a good thing. Architecture has got to be about people realizing their dreams! Most of the buildings that are going up in big cities these days, there can't be any sort of dream behind them! Take the Shell building, that's my favourite building here in Berlin. There's obviously a dream behind that, whoever it was really dared to dream up something beautiful. Not everybody is as gifted as that, but there is an absence of that quality from so many buildings today. Architecture is to do with courage too . . . and that's what bugs me about Frankfurt: it's so spiritless, the things they put up, it's all about greed and profit. That one bank building in New York, with the angled silver roof, the City Corp building, just one building like that in Frankfurt would transform the whole skyline. But there isn't one. Well, OK, that's a bit of an exaggeration, but it would be at least bearable if there was just one playful element there. But no, it's just these wretched blocks.

*First published in* Quaderns, *No. 176, September 1987*

# PART IV

# He paints his socks off

Christian Rothmann is the only painter I've ever made an emergency stop for. There was a bus coming in the other direction, and as I was passing it, I noticed on its side panel a yellow figure with thin legs (or feelers?) that I'd spotted the day before on a poster site under the Yorck bridges, when I'd caused chaos by hanging a U-turn in heavy traffic.

That yellow guy had something. It was as funny as my favourite comic character Krazy Kat; it was descended from the scurrilous forms of Miró, and from the melancholy or even tragic conceptions of Paul Klee, but at the same time it was unique and particular, and it was also, I thought, brilliantly painted.

By now I know the painter a bit, and because I also have a couple of his paintings in front of me every day, I don't need to go via the Yorck bridges quite so often. (Where even today, a year later, at the foot of an old iron bridge prop, there's a cheeky little spin-off of the yellow figure hanging around, who makes me chuckle every time.)

It would be wrong to think, though, that Christian Rothmann is a humorist or caricaturist. He is a regular painter. He paints his socks off. When I picture him in front of a canvas, I think of him as 'someone who shows himself in his true colours every day'. OK, so do a lot of painters, but not many with such joy, lightness and density. Why is that? Maybe it's not just down to him, maybe this is as much about me: could it be that his painting matches my tastes to a t? In other words; what he paints (or more the way he paints) pleases me so much because the content (and form) is *bound* to appeal to me. That's right, isn't it: you like what gives you pleasure. My liking for Christian Rothmann's paintings reflects my liking for a lot of other things too. Such as?

For instance, I like series: similar themes being rehearsed in a particular form. In comic strips, in thrillers, in games of soccer or baseball (and other sports too), in blues, and in rock'n'roll. In movies, sure. I like the sense of freedom that you get with a series, from using a set form, using all the space it gives you to explore every conceivable variation, going to the limits and then, of course, beyond them. As a concept, it's like play, and I love playing.

I love colour, especially in the form of new boxes of water-colours, unopened packets of pens and crayons, the colour charts in paint-shops, samples of carpet or cloth or wallpaper or metallic car paints. I can spend hours gazing at the window displays in art shops, admiring the palettes of oil, crayon, acrylic and chalk. Not because I'm a painter manqué (though I am, I admit it), but because I love colour as possibility, as a possible life: as something waiting to be tried out, used, arranged. Here too, there's the idea of play. And a sense of freedom, a different one, more obvious and even more pleasurable. (And when I do succumb, and buy the box of water-colours or felt-tips or chalks, the greatest pleasure is stepping out their domain, the freedom these colours offer me: on a sheet of white paper I put a dab of every water-colour, thinly at the edge of the page, thicker in the middle, or I use felt-tips to make a grid of colour, like Paul Klee's. Sometimes I write the name of the colour in the colour, if there are several shades close together, that's a particular pleasure for me.) What it all means, I don't know, I'm trying to find out.

I love foreign alphabets. There are no more beautiful 'signs' for me than writing I can't read. Hieroglyphs make me wild. I can lose myself in the exotic forms of a Balinese calendar, a Chinese menu, an Arabic newspaper. If I see a film with Japanese subtitles (written vertically up the side!) I spend more time looking at the letters than the pictures. As a child, I tried to invent additional letters for our Roman alphabet, or additional numerals, if we didn't have the decimal or duodecimal system.

I could go on about the things I relate to in Christian Rothmann's paintings, all the pleasures I associate them with. But that's not the point. The point is to describe his work, and after my long preamble that's what I've now come round to.

Christian Rothmann is an explorer of unknown colour alphabets. He paints buried continents of new signs. He's a map-maker of unknown territories full of bewildering forms. A tour guide through previously unseen grammars of images. He invents games for which no one knows the rules, but which straight away make sense. On paper and canvas he conjugates colours and forms.

He is a linguist of colour. I recommend an emergency stop.

*First published in* Loose Band *(exhibition catalogue), published by Z-Art and the Art Department of Kreuzberg, Berlin, August 1998*

## Winter Märchen

When you film or photograph a place, do you have a different relationship to it than if you'd just stood there a while and looked? Do you get a proprietorial feeling? What does the person who's 'got the picture' of a place, take with him? What does he leave behind?

It's a different matter, I imagine, for a painter, who gives something to a place rather than takes something. A writer, whose story is set in a certain place, doesn't take anything from it either: the reader still has to see it in his own inner eye. But a photographer often slinks away from the scene like a criminal; that's how I've felt when taking pictures myself, and I've felt like that at times when looking at pictures other people have taken. What about a film-maker? Isn't he a painter, writer and photographer all rolled into one? What does he do to a place? What does he give, what does he take away? What's left of a place when he's finished with it?

Those questions suggested themselves to me when I saw Mario Ambrosius's pictures of Berlin, and discovered two shots of *Wings of Desire* among them that he'd taken from a screening of the film. Right next to them is a photograph from the winter of 1990/1991: such a lot has changed. First and foremost, the Wall has gone! But the angel Cassiel will always be walking beside the Wall with old Homer. If that had been two photographs, it would be a straightforward matter: before and after. But the film seems to record things and places in a different way to photography. In a photo, the before and after is immanent, both are always contained in it, just by virtue of the way a photograph is a split second between past and future. Not a film. A film has its own time structure. It tells a story, and in that story time and place are both subordinated to the story. Does that mean that films are always unfair to their location, that they always, wrongfully, assert their own unique time, the continuous present of a film?

Just lately I walked across the Potsdamer Platz in snow, right across it, through the Wall. Even though it's now gone, you still have to cross it. The huge empty terrain gave me the feeling of *terra incognita*. Setting foot in Alaska or Tierra del Fuego couldn't have been any more of an adventure. The Berolina Circus is there, where a circus would have been quite inconceivable previously. (Ambrosius has a picture of it, I just happened to see.) The circus makes the place seem even more deserted than it already is. The sky is as grey as it only ever gets in Berlin. I stop. Time passes, I don't have a camera with me. The Potsdamer Platz isn't mine, I am its. The magnetic railway will soon be gone too. The road, winding its rather higgledy-piggledy way, will follow a different, straighter course. The old Huth building, all alone now, will soon be flanked by the head office of Mercedes. And as I stand there, time passes 'before my very eyes', the time of this place, far vaster and more powerful than my own little time. 'That great time of places', I think, that would silence all pictures and film images, I think with awe in my heart.

Maybe that's where the injustice that a film can do to a place resides: it renders their 'big time' invisible by claiming that its own story is more to the point. And maybe you can define the petty larceny of so many photographs in a similar way: they thoughtlessly lift a fraction of a second, which will be missing from the place for all eternity, and without which it will always be disfigured.

That suggests a sort of morality for photographers and film-makers to do with places: never to impose their split second or their story on a place, without paying homage to the so-much greater story and longer time of the place. If they don't do that, you will be shown up, because a camera always works in two ways at once: it shows whatever it's pointed at, but it also exposes (in both senses of the word) the view of the photographer or cameraman. A book of pictures doesn't just show a place, it offers an insight ('an open book', no less) into the heart of the photographer, just as a film doesn't just offer its 'takes', but also shows the 'take on things' of whoever is making it.

If that take is superficial or impatient or merely curious or sensationalist or deprecating or negative or even contemptuous – it shows. Lack of respect shows.

But so does affection too.

And with that, I've come to what I want to say about Mario

Ambrosius's pictures: they don't just show me Berlin, with all the drama of the change that has just taken place, and will continue to take place far into the future, they also show me what's behind the camera, the love and affection and respect for the place 'Berlin', that shows itself most clearly in the distance that it preserves. It's a view you can trust. It has let itself be penetrated by the grey winter light; it's gone a long way on foot, it wandered around at night, it went looking, and when it found something, it dared to hesitate and if need be, to wait. It had encountered Berlin.

Mario Ambrosius has done more than steal time from this place.

*First published in: Mario Ambrosius*, Berlin – Winter Märchen
Without Walls, *Berlin, August 1991*

# Eye colours

I was going to write about 'colour', about colours in films and the connection between 'colour', 'beauty' and 'truth'.

My effort landed in the bin, and that's where it's going to stay. It was trying to do too much. It wanted to argue a connection between all the different things I felt watching the retrospective on colour at the Astor cinema this past fortnight. And the way it gets when you're out to prove something instead of merely describing it, the proof became the point of the whole thing, and the thing you should have been describing merely ends up crushed under the sheer weight of evidence.

Forget it.

I have to face it: the *Taz* editor is about to call, and I'll have to appear in my true colours: no piece on colour. By trying to isolate the phenomenon of colour, I made myself colour-blind. So what now? Maybe I can invoke other connections between 'truth' and 'beauty', and work some 'colour' into them that is still fresh in my mind from the glut of films I've seen in the course of the recent festival. Yes, maybe I can even define the 'colour of films' as 'moments of truth' and 'beauty', like the shock of watching an actor or actress and suddenly being so moved, it feels as though you're sitting opposite them in life and could see through his (or her) eyes right into the soul. Those 'colours of the inner eye' would be the truest and most beautiful colours in a film, whether it be Technicolor, Trucolor, Eastmancolor or just black and white. Here are some instances of eye colours that I saw in the festival:

In Yasujiro Ozu's *Akibiyori*, throughout the entire film and in every one of the actors, but most particularly in Setsuko Hara's eyes, and most clearly in the last shot of the film, as she's sitting alone in her empty apartment following her daughter's wedding, staring into space, with a happy smile and at the same time crying in her desolation . . .

In the two films by Agnes Varda, in the cheerful, boundless and implacable honesty of Jane Birkin in *Jane B. by Agnes V.*, and also in her patient despair about growing old in *Kung Fu Master*, and there too most of all in the final scene, where Jane is talking to her daughter Charlotte with such fierce intensity that you wonder how the camera got to be there at all . . .

In the Soviet film *The Commissar*, in all three lead actors, in the cheerfulness of the Jewish craftsman Rolan Bykov and his wife Raisa Nedashkovskaya, and in the breathtaking 'humanization' process of the soldier Nonna Mordjukova, whom I will always remember proudly laying her arm round the cradle of her newborn baby . . .

In Derek Jarman's *The Last of England*, when Tilda Swinton appears and tells you more in a mysterious 'wedding dance' than a whole novel could . . .

In Soleiman Cisse's *Yeelen*, in the faces of the old mother and her son when they say goodbye . . .

In Reinhard Hauff's *Linie 1*, as Ilona Schulz sings her first song on the subway . . .

In James Brooks's *Broadcast News*, when the tiny, feisty news producer Holly Hunter gives up a relationship with a man she's really interested in, because he's guilty of a fiddle that must happen thousands of times every day on American television. (I'm inclined to see this film as one of the most intelligent critiques of the American entertainment industry, though with not quite the stringency of Martin Scorsese's hopelessly misunderstood *King of Comedy*.) It's a pity there's a fake ending tacked onto *Broadcast News* that takes the whole thing back, not unlike the ending of *The Commissar*, incidentally. In both films, you can tell that the non-ending was a condition of their being made at all.

That was the colour palette of the last few days that lives in my memory, those were my moments of truth. I don't want to do anything more than list them here, because otherwise I'd run the risk of starting to try and prove something once more. If the editorial people at *Taz* managed to get hold of photographs of some of these actors and actresses, that would make me very happy.

*First appeared in* Tageszeitung (Taz), *24 February 1988*

# A step ahead of the times
Conversation about photography, painting and film with Paul
Püschel and Jan Thorn-Prikker

QUESTION: *In the foreword to your book of photographs* Written in the
West *you talk about the connection between film and photography. It
only occurred to me afterwards what an odd title* Written in the West *is
for a book of photographs. Shouldn't it have been 'Seen in the West'?*

WIM WENDERS: I chose the title because I noticed that the pictures I took
in America all had writing in them. If you flick through the book, you'll
see there's something written in almost every picture. The landscape quite
literally asks to be read. I think it was that more than anything else that
made me want to take photographs of it. And that's why I called the book
*Written in the West.*

*You once wrote: 'It's not my job to express myself in words. My job is
seeing, and then showing what I've seen . . . in pictures and films.' Don't
words in photographs pose a threat? Shouldn't pictures be able to exist
without any words in them?*

I found something really moving about those words, those scraps of sense,
that were once put there – particularly in the context of that Western
landscape. Most of the words and sentences were just fragmentary, and
now completely lacking in meaning. The script is actually as much of a
ruin as most of the buildings you see there. I find the collision of that once
mythic Western landscape with those isolated scraps of writing, the
juxtaposition of those two pictorial elements the best way of conveying
the landscape in pictures. Once, around the end of the last century, and at
the beginning of this one, it was where the future was supposed to be. It
was pioneer country. And now it's become a wasteland, where the
American dream of the West is expressed in a few forgotten words.
They're like a sad commentary on the landscape. The picture in front of us
has a sign in it that reads 'Western World Development'. It's obvious that

not an acre of it has been developed for decades. It's just somebody's dream of a city, and that label's all that's left of the dream, an epitaph really.

*The pictures of the American photographer Walker Evans, who has influenced you a lot, have two distinct sides to them. Not only is he an outstanding documentary photographer, in his later pictures he succeeded in making autonomous photographs out of words and letters, sometimes fragments of letters. He manages to convert, or to return script into image and design. With him, the written word isn't just a word, it conveys rich and multiple meanings because of how it looks.*

I think that might be the biggest contribution to contemporary art of American culture: its discovery of writing as a pictorial element. That never existed before. The Americans have come up with incredibly beautiful styles too. 'Signwriting' used to be a real craft. The signwriters who moved out West to put up big and bold and beautiful signs everywhere, I see them as being like the forerunners of pop art.

*So you think pop art took up something that was already an American tradition and just gave it more prominence?*

Yes, more than anything it quoted. The best examples aren't even in pop art – which I think was an exploitative kind of thing – they're just standing around abandoned in the American landscape. I think Walker Evans did more to develop a feeling for that popular American art-form than Robert Indiana or Andy Warhol ever did. He may not have been the first to see what potential there was for pictures in the American landscape, but he was certainly the first to find a clear language for it in his pictures, to find a form for the American landscape.

*In the foreword to your book of photographs you say: 'For me the American West is a place in decline', and a little later, where you're talking about signs you say: 'signs in the landscape are becoming less and less visible. Previously people used to drive through that enormous terrain, then there were trains from which you could view it at a different speed, and after that there were aeroplanes, and certainly by that time it had become impossible to see the individual signs in the landscape properly.' Does the observation of things have to do with the speed of perception, the speed with which people travel through these vast terrains? I'm asking because cars, trains and aeroplanes play such a big part in all your films.*

Yes, of course it affects the way you see if you're on foot somewhere and if you're driving and taking pictures out of the car window, which is what most people do, they don't even stop, and if you fly right over it and reach your destination – ping – and you haven't even journeyed to the place, you only arrived there. And of course it's getting more and more like that. People nowadays only ever arrive, they've stopped travelling. They take a picture to convince themselves afterwards that they were ever there at all.

*So are your films a kind of plea for those forgotten landscapes, things, situations and people? Do you see film-making as an archival activity?*

Without question. Sometimes you only notice afterwards, but sometimes it's done quite consciously. I remember how in *The American Friend* we had Bruno Ganz live in a house by the harbour front because we happened to hear the whole terrace was about to be demolished. In *The Goalkeeper's Fear of the Penalty* there's a building where Wittgenstein once lived, again because we heard that might be under threat too. Looking at it like that, there are similar examples in just about every film of mine. The fact that something is due to go is always a good reason to include it in a scene. *Wings of Desire* is full of examples. Almost none of our locations exists any more. Starting with the bridge where the motorcyclist dies. That's gone. The place where we had the circus is now a park. No need to mention Potsdamer Platz. Or the Wall either. The whole film suddenly turned into an archive for things that aren't around any more. Films that don't call themselves documentaries, feature films, do that to an amazing degree. In the next century, I think we'll get a better idea of the 1930s in America from watching Howard Hawk's comedies than some documentaries. In the long run, feature films will be the truly important documentaries of our time.

*Can we go back to the connection between films and photography. Susan Sontag once wrote: 'Photography is preserving, is safeguarding things.' That safeguarding aspect of photography is clearly important to you. But Susan Sontag also talked about another side of photography. She showed that the taking of any photograph has an element of violence in it. You cut something out of its context. You turn something living into a static image. So photographs are acts of affection, of cherishing and safe-guarding things, scenes and people, but at the same time acts of violence. How do you see that working out?*

I would say that's how things can be, without hesitation. Yes, every time you photograph or film something, there can be something violent or intrusive about it. But you need to keep that in proportion. I would say that in filming or photographing something, you both document it and cut it out of its surrounding reality to put it in your frame. But at the same time, quite uncannily, every act of filming or photographing also documents what's going on *behind* the camera. Every picture documents the attitude which the photographer or cameraman brings to it. German has this word 'Einstellung' (take). A take is an attempt at getting a particular scene 'into shot'. But at the same time, it's what remains outside, namely the individual 'take' of the film-maker on his subject. People either don't understand that, or they refuse to believe that a camera works in two directions at once. But that's the way it is. In films, you observe that very clearly. You notice very quickly whether a film loves the things that are in it or despises them. In single-shot photography, it's not quite so easy to tell. But you still pick up on it. If you live with photographs, you always end up knowing whether the photographer was in love with what he was taking, or was indifferent to it, or even hated it. You get all three.

There are photographers who specialize in taking pictures of things they dislike, and there are photographers who only take things they have a close relationship with. That relationship can be very solicitous. So I have to disagree with Susan Sontang to that extent. I don't think a photograph has to be an act of violence, a photograph can also be a very tender act, or – what about this as a compromise: an act of tender violence.

*I want to go back to Walker Evans again. I can't think of any greater love or affection for subjects, no photographer who effaces himself as much behind the things he takes. At the same time, though, his affection for them seems absolutely clear. How does he do that?*

That's a moral question really. It's a question you have to answer each time you take a picture – every day and whoever you are. I think you could say as a photographer Walker Evans was a great moralist. Every picture shows his great 'regard' for his subject. With other people, it's not like that at all. Especially when you look at the bastardization of photography, to advertise God knows what. Evans's kind of respect has become increasingly rare. That might have something to do with the incredible inflation of images we're exposed to. That tends to make you either indifferent to the subject, or actually contemptuous of it. For instance, that gorgeous landscape on the Arizona/Utah border, Monument Valley, that someone like the Indian photographer Edward Curtis photographed with awe and astonishment. That's now the landscape you know from the cigarette ads. It's been so desecrated by photography that it ought to be left alone for a hundred years so that someone can actually see that landscape again. Photography can be a horribly violent act, it's true.

*Would I be right in thinking that another American photographer, Robert Frank, has influenced your way of looking at things?*

Yes, you would and he has. People always refer to him as an American photographer, but what he was was the European photographer who loved America. *Par excellence.* He had a love-hate relationship with America, which is the European view, so to speak: a mixture of fascination and alarm. His pictures express that divided attitude very clearly.

*Is another reason why you value Robert Frank because he's a photographer of inner unrest, because he's always on the move, because he's a travel photographer?*

Yes, surely. But I think that was always a part of photography from the beginning. Half of all photographers were travel photographers. The invention of photography was always going to be bound up with travelling. But to get back to Robert Frank. There's someone who sees a lot of things. Moments that you or I might miss altogether, or only catch in hindsight, he sees in time to capture them on film. He's really quite unique because he seems to be able to take pictures out of the corners of his eyes, as it were. There's not many can do that.

*You once said you would like to be able to film just like opening your eyes and catching some fleeting impression. Isn't that what Robert Frank's photographs do? You can't imagine him using a tripod. You once called Robert Frank a modest photographer, who doesn't like to draw attention to himself, who likes to retire behind whatever thing seems important to him. Is that something a film-maker can do?*

The difference with films is that you're trying to tell a story at the same time. And telling a story makes that modest look very hard, it gets terribly in the way, and gives you this headache: a storyteller by definition is someone who puffs himself up, by claiming to be inventing something.

That's the dilemma with every film story: the extent to which it makes it impossible to look at something actual. You make something up: a story, set in a place, a city or a landscape, and sometimes it happens that what you've made up makes it impossible to look out into the landscape. All you're able to look at is your invention. The landscape behind it just gets used. And that's what a photographer has to try and avoid.

*As a director you're open to a lot of different things. You've worked with the novelist Peter Handke, and you've taken on photography. You're a good photographer yourself.*

There's another thing you need to take into account as well, and that's painting. In the director's bind between wanting to tell a story and wanting just to see, painting is another source of experience. In painting, seeing and telling a story collide in a different way than they do for the photographer and the film-maker. It's a kind of third possibility.

*Can you talk about a painter who matters to you?*

The obvious example is Edward Hopper, especially the city paintings. He always had this particular starting point, even where his pictures sometimes look universal and fairly abstract. There is a famous painting of a street in New York with a barber's shop in the middle. For me that painting stands in a very exciting relation to film and to photography. I've seen it many times. It's in the Whitney Museum in New York. I often went there, and each time I thought, next time I visit, the picture will have changed: maybe there will be someone crossing the street, say. It's a painting you expect will suddenly jerk into life and change, have different light, something. It's a painting in suspense, or in suspension. It has great affinities with photography. Though actually it's less stiff than a photograph.

*With Hopper I always thought he's about to tell a story, something is about to happen or has just happened, like in the cinema. His painting of the cinema usherette is fantastic. It's a painting about a different medium. I've never seen anything else like that. It's like the promise of a picture that would produce other pictures. It's a painting I can only imagine coming from America. Like Hopper's paintings of filling stations too. Painting something humdrum like that, without being afraid of banality – I really admire that. They are paintings with no interest in profundity, but they aren't superficial either.*

I completely agree with you. An Edward Hopper painting is like the opening paragraph of a story. A car will drive up to a filling station, and the driver will have a bullet in his belly. They are like the beginning of American films.

*Pictures like that have to do something to guard against triviality and banality. They need to have some ingredient that permits them to survive as an image of the time from which they came. A picture needs to outlast its time. Image needs some kind of seal or lacquer to make it last.*

That gets you to thinking about art and time, which is important in photography as well. Those artists I think of as my 'contemporaries' actually need to be slightly ahead of their time, so that at any given moment you can see the whole of the present, but with a little extra. 'Now' isn't just evoked, but already understood. In the last few days I got that feeling from the Anselm Kiefer show at the Berlin Nationalgalerie. I thought: there's a contemporary. Someone who paints today in that incredible way, and always a step ahead of the rest of us. I think Anselm Kiefer is quite right to resist the political interpretations of his paintings. You don't even need them, to understand that those are contemporary paintings. They show you quite unmistakeably that he's a German painter, and this is a show happening in 1991 in Germany.

*Isn't it the obvious thing to call Kiefer a painter of German mythology? Someone who's able to look back a long way and refracts what he sees in the mirror of the 1000-year Reich.\* The reaction to Kiefer, in the States in particular, is to see him as the painter of German history and German mythology. But you seem to see a different time-scale in Kiefer's work.*

It's always one of those things with myths. I think reading myths for their 'application' or 'significance' is an incredibly boring thing to do. But to see myths as something valued at all times, including today, because of their mythic force, which remains effective regardless of any particular time or how it likes to see itself, I think that is important. In other words, understanding myths not as history, but for their force *now*, today. That's what sets Kiefer apart as a painter. Not that he re-heats some old myths, but that he has an eye for myths in the reality of today, that makes him a 'true contemporary'.

*In front of Kiefer's painting,* Mesopotamia, Land of Two Rivers *there are his lead bomber planes. When I look at those two works, 'Mesopotamia' and 'Bombers' in the wake of the Gulf War, there's a coincidence like you might get on television – an artist's work formulating a political situation long before it became reality with the Gulf War. Although, actually, that's a superficial interpretation. The arrangement of the two works was a happy accident, and I ask myself as I look at it suspiciously, am I denying an aspect of Kiefer's artistry here, has he intuited something far ahead of the rest of us, or has time itself arranged something that he couldn't possibly have known when he created those works?*

I think time has done something he's probably not too happy about, because it's far too close to a tabloid version of history. You would be able to see his planes better, absurd though it might sound, had there not been the Gulf War. You would be better able to respond to them. But because there has been the war, and there are the planes, you can't easily resist that tabloid version of things. But if you don't try and resist it, just stand in front of them and take them on, both the tabloid thing, and those machines and their freight – then you suddenly know you're standing in

---

*The Third Reich (Trans.).

front of something from now. You look at them differently than you would if you were in a museum looking at things from the 1960s and 70s and 80s.

*Are there other painters you have thought about a lot? Are there painters who figure in your work at all?*

In my new film, *To the End of the World*, which is set in the year 2000 and is a kind of science fiction film, there are several painters who were very important to me as I was making it, like Vermeer. It's hard to explain the exact connection, suffice it to say the film is about the future of seeing, to put it crudely. There are several painters in it, Vermeer, the Impressionists, but seeing as it isn't ready yet, I'd rather not talk about it any more at this stage.

*First appeared in* Kulturchronik, *August 1991*

PART V

# For the city that dreams

I missed the whole thing. It's hardly possible to be any further away from Berlin than I am right now, in the Western Australian desert. There are no newspapers, no radio, TV only once or twice a week in some motel somewhere, and even then only local stations and what they can get on satellite – which isn't much. So far there's been nothing on Berlin at all, it's just too far away. I get my news by telephone, when I'm lucky enough to get a connection. My office in Berlin faxed me two pictures: one of them shows people apparently dancing on the Wall (just a couple of hundred yards from where I live, according to the caption), and on the other there's a man sitting on the Wall, attacking the concrete with hammer and chisel. The pictures have the quality of bad photocopies, with strong contrasts and little in the way of recognizable detail. For a long time I looked at them with tears in my eyes. Yes, I felt homesick, and that isn't a feeling I have very often.

A couple of days ago we ran into a crazy guy, a hermit who lived in a cave. It was early in the morning, but he was already completely plastered. He came from Lithuania and spoke a bit of German. He raised glass after glass to Berlin, and yelled, over the Wagner on his ghetto-blaster: 'No more Walls! No more walls anywhere!'

I experienced the events in Berlin with the same naivety with which a child might try to imagine, say, a foreign country. I had those two fuzzy pictures, nothing else, but they showed me more than two thousand or even two million clear photographs: they let me dream. I have Bob Dylan on the earpiece of my Walkman. He's singing: 'Ring them bells, you hear them, for the city that dreams . . .' I hope Berlin's dreams haven't turned into nightmares by the time I get back in mid-December. Too many images give you a headache. Worst still: too many images of yourself.

I may have missed everything, but my feeling is I haven't really missed a thing.

*Faxed from Turkey Creek, Western Australia to* Libération *on 15 November 1989, and published there on 24 November 1989*

# Not alone in a big house

'L'identité culturelle Européenne', 'the cultural identity of Europe'. . . I want to try and think of these three words separately and together, so that I can get some kind of picture in my head and some feeling in my heart, after all the opinions and descriptions and historical meditations and philosophical analyses I've read and listened to these past few days.

The only thing to help me on my way was the subtitle: 'L'Europe vue d'ailleurs', 'Europe seen from elsewhere'. Seeing, now, seeing is something that interests me. Seeing is my job: I make films. Seeing Europe instead of analysing it, that's what I'd like to do here.

'Europe seen from elsewhere . . .' Why ask me about the perspective on Europe 'from elsewhere', if not because I've lived and worked for seven years in the USA. That's the only thing that qualifies me to open my mouth here. And perhaps it's not a bad justification either, because it was in America that I first began to define myself as a European in what I did. 'I'm a European film-maker' is what I said. And after calling myself that, and accepting that I'd never become 'an American film-maker', and after deciding that because of my self-definition, but also to further it, I would return home, I said: 'I'm going back to Europe.' I didn't say 'to Germany' or 'to France' but 'to Europe'. Was it just the distance that caused me to say that, was it because, from America, the countries in Europe are all so tiny, they just blur into one another? I don't think so. It wasn't to do with distance or geography. There was something I was missing in America, so profoundly and urgently and painfully that it wasn't enough to say: 'I'm going back to Germany or back to France.' No, my destination had to be Europe, it took that word to encompass what I needed.

But then why had I never felt such a need before, when I'd been living 'in Europe'? Why did Europe become visible to me 'from a distance', not when it was all around me? Often you have to lose something to be able to appreciate its worth. So what, if anything, had I lost while I was in

America? An 'identity'? Whose? And why? Because I couldn't become an American, or, worse, because I actually had?

Let me start again, and try to get a better purchase on these words I'm using. 'Identity': something that relieves your anxiety, your fear of the void. Lack of identity: chasms of fear and dread opening up in front of you. Loss of identity: despair and death. That makes 'identity' a kind of weapon, a kind of protection, armour, the ground under your feet, security, pride and strength. Fine. Now then, the two words in combination: 'cultural identity', what might they mean? A feeling of being at one with a culture? And how to define 'culture' if not as 'spiritual sustenance'? Whatever enables us to survive morally and physically. Therefore, what I felt in America was lack of identity: insufficient spiritual sustenance.

It appears to me now that the 'German identity' that I took with me to the States didn't offer adequate protection. It couldn't hold out against the temptation of America. Luckily, then, I had another set of clothes, another skin, that afforded better protection. Under my German waistcoat, I wore my European shirt of mail – if you'll allow me to speak figuratively – woven from a number of languages, cultures, frontiers, regions, wars and friendships. Those are all the things Americans don't have. They are alone, they think they make up the whole world. On the one hand, their feeling of superiority and, on the other, their inferiority complex stem directly from that. They have a different problem: that of living alone in a big house. In Europe we do the opposite. The experience of all living under one roof has caused us no end of grief and turmoil historically, but today it's a source of strength and richness. All the various national identities are able to live and prosper under that one mighty shield.

Let me start over again. I referred to my European profession. There is, let me tell you, a European art-form and a common language *par excellence*: the European film. The clearest manifestation of 'European identity' is in the cinema, more than in all the other arts, with their different national traditions. Let me call to mind some great European artists: Eisenstein, Dreyer, Lang, Renoir, Rossellini, Buñuel, Truffaut, Tarkovsky, and some contemporaries, Fellini, Antonioni, Godard, Bergmann, Angelopoulos, Oliveira . . . where would the list end? Only the European cinema is capable of maintaining dignity and morality in a savage cacophony of images, is capable of stemming the avalanche that's heading our way, in the new era of electronic images, of satellite and cable communications. The inflation of images which will in time give us the same headaches about reality and identity that already characterize American images and American TV, can only be opposed by our European images, our common art and language, our European cinema, which we must do everything in our power to protect and defend.

I have no interest in defining that art or that 'European identity'; the main thing is: it exists. These past two days, the European identity has often been invoked, sometimes as mysterious and elusive, at others as clear and self-evident. I wouldn't mind if it remained inexplicable, so long as it could also continue to operate and radiate. I hope that we all remain French, German, English, Irish, Polish, Portuguese, Greek or Swedish, but still continue to share that inexplicable and self-evident something else: the privilege of living together under the one roof of the European house.

*First published in*: Europe sans Rivage, *Editions Albin Michel,*
*Paris, 1988*

# On the future of European cinema
## Conversation with Marcel Bergmann and Bernhard Beutler

QUESTION: *In the last few years, while you were working on* To the End of the World, *you took your title quite literally, and went from one world trip to another. In spite of that – or perhaps because of it – the question: How much has German unification and the far-reaching political transformation of Europe affected your work and that of other European film-makers?*

WIM WENDERS: That remains to be seen. The European cinema will reflect those political changes, but it's currently in a position in which its very survival is under threat. At the moment I'm working in an organization called the 'European Cinema Society' made up of 59 European directors, producers, actors and scriptwriters. It's not just some EC grouping, but represents Europe in the broadest sense. We have directors from every country from Turkey to Iceland, Poland and the USSR. Right now we're in the process of changing our society to a 'European Film Academy' on the model of the 'Academy of Motion Pictures' in Hollywood. We want it to be a sovereign group, not a sectional interest group for producers or distributors, or any sort of trade union, more a kind of conscience of the European film industry, a source of moral authority. We want it not to be narrowly political but to represent the interests of the European cinema and European directors in the widest sense. One of the things we do is preside over the awarding – now for the fourth time – of the Felix, the European Film Prize, in Berlin.

*As the unification of Europe looms ever larger, political and economic interests seem to be pushing the cultural sector more and more into the background. What opportunities do you see for film culture to assist in the realization of the European ideal – say on the basis of what you're doing with the 'European Film Society'?*

What preoccupies us at the moment is maximizing the audience we can get for the films that receive the European Film Prize. We had the idea of that prize as a kind of European Oscar, to help promote European cinema as a whole. We'd like to invest our full authority – 60 of the biggest names in the European cinema – to get those films distributed in every European country. We have a prize for the 'Best European Film' and another for the 'Best Newcomer', and we're putting together a plan to get our prizewinners – and especially the newcomers – to benefit from the individual and collective reputation as members of the European Film Academy.

*Are you trying to forge an identity for the European cinema, or has the situation really deteriorated to one of bare survival?*

I think the question at the moment isn't really about what the European cinema is. Everybody has their own views about that anyway. It's more a fight to get an audience for European films. In the current set-up, there's absolutely no guarantee of that. If, say, *Terminator* is launched with 65 copies in Paris, that implies the loss of fully 30 or 40 cinemas to other films, including European films. That's the kind of thing we're up against. Small things are threatened with extinction, and unfortunately the European cinema is pretty small these days, or it's become small. Which isn't to say that we're about to knuckle under.

*In your new film,* To the End of the World, *you have a character on the run from the Nazis. Here in Lyons, the city where Klaus Barbie acquired his grisly reputation, that's something one has to think about every day as a German. Was it really important to you to have your film, which takes us past the year 2000, still featuring that bit of our past?*

What you're referring to is a little bit of the story of Edith (Jeanne Moreau), a woman who met her future husband when they were both still children, and had to flee Europe by way of Lisbon. She tells the story in such an underplayed sort of way, just as part of her life, that it isn't really an issue in the rest of the film.

*But perhaps people in Lyons would tend to overreact to it.*

Yes, perhaps they're hypersensitive here, which one could understand.

What I liked about that bit of biography was the opposite really, that it was so straightforward, didn't have any implications or significance and wasn't picked up again later either. It was just her life story: a French girl fleeing in the late 1930s, meets a German boy who's lost both his parents. They fall in love. That's all.

*On 9 November 1989, when the Berlin Wall came down, you were away in Australia. Did your work on that project of yours, in which you examine very fundamental issues concerning death and dreams and the boundaries of scientific progress and so forth, did that completely eclipse the events in Berlin for you? Or what was it about that time that most moved you?*

I would have dropped everything and got on a plane if I hadn't happened to be at a point I'd been trying to reach for the past ten years, namely to get my film *To the End of the World* off the ground. So finally I reach that point and it's all starting to come together, and suddenly there are these incredible things happening in Germany, and most of all in Berlin. If it had all been my own production, if it hadn't required so much backing and so on, then I would simply have got up and said: All right guys, we have to stop, there are more important things happening! But with that mammoth production, and with so many obligations and responsibilities, that wasn't on. Maybe it was the very distance from which I was following the events of November 89 in Berlin that made them so extraordinarily emotional for me. I had to imagine everything for myself. Over there in the desert there wasn't any television, so I couldn't see any pictures from Berlin at all. All there was was phone-calls via satellite, and a few very bad quality faxed photographs. That was all I got. Everything had to happen in my own imagination, so to speak. At that time I met a man, a settler, who lived in some sort of cave. That guy had a radio, a shortwave radio. He was a drinker of the kind you sometimes meet in the barren wastes of the Australian desert. He knew something of what was going on in Berlin, because he'd picked it up on his shortwave. He had Beethoven's 'Ode to Joy' going on his ghetto-blaster the whole time. That morning he was sitting out in the unbelievable heat, singing *'Freude schöner Götterfunken'* at the top of his voice. And at the same time blubbing like a baby. I sat down with him and started blubbing too. Because there wasn't that whole inundation of images that you had in Germany, where you got to see everything ten thousand times, it was a completely different, more internalized sort of experience for me. I had to picture it all for myself. Or perhaps I should say: I had the privilege. Of picturing.

*You recently said at a press conference that you're now completely fed up with travelling, that the sight of aeroplanes make you sick, and your next film is going be made on foot or, at the most, on a bicycle. Does that mean you want to film in Europe, even in Germany?*

I'm going to make my next film in Berlin again. At the moment we're living in a time that is clearly historic. That's widely understood in Berlin, maybe not quite so much in the former West Germany. You can feel it in the streets and bars: people sense they're living through an exceptional period. In the last couple of years the whole reunification was too unbelievable, it's taken until now for it to really sink in. And to convert that into a reality, a new perspective, is something we've only begun to do. That's why I wanted to make a film in Berlin, starring mainly children and young people, with Otto Sander in the lead, who was the angel who remained in *Wings of Desire*. It's a kind of sequel, in a light-hearted sort of way.

*The conversation took place in Lyons in October 1991.*
*First publication*

## Talk about Germany

Good morning.

To talk at all is to talk about oneself, whether it be implicitly, through choice of words, grammar and accent, or explicitly, in giving a personal opinion, talking from personal experience or about one's self. I'm going to be quite explicit and talk about myself. I can only 'talk about Germany' by talking about the German in me. I don't have much to say about 'the Germans'; in fact, I don't believe that 'they' exist.

Just as my name isn't really 'Wim' Wenders. It's Ernst Wilhelm Wenders.

I was conceived in the winter of 1944/5, the last of the War, in the Eiffel Mountains, and was born in August 1945 in Düsseldorf on the Rhine, to Dr Heinrich Wenders and his wife Martha, a week after the bombing of Hiroshima and Nagasaki, and on the day of the Japanese capitulation. I like to think that that would have been the headline on the day of my birth if – I don't know – 'we' had started printing newspapers again by then.

When my father went to the registry office to have me entered as 'Wim' an official objected that that wasn't a German name, so my father was forced to put 'Wilhelm' instead. My middle name was Ernst, after my godfather. For some mysterious reason, that name was put first, so even now, when I go to the States, say, I'm registered as 'Ernst double-U', not even Wilhelm.

I spent my early years in the house of my grandfather, the apothecary Wilhelm Wenders. He ran the Pfalz chemist's shop on the Kaiserwerther Strasse. All around it had been bombed, but that building had escaped unscathed. My earliest memories are of rubble. Heaps of rubble. Chimney stacks pointing up at the sky like fingers. A tram weaving its way through mountains of rubble. That was the world. As a child you take it as you find it.

After that, we lived in Koblenz for four years, on the banks of the River Mosel. That was where I started going to school, to the Moselweiss Elementary School. Then we moved back to Düsseldorf, and I went to Urdenbach Elementary, and after that to the gymnasium in Benrath. The boys' gymnasium was provisionally housed in Benrath Castle. A little while ago I was invited to the Elysée Palace, and spotted a picture of 'my school' in President Mitterand's study, and proudly pointed out 'my classroom' window. In the picture it was still part of a stable block.

I spent my last years of gymnasium in the Ruhrgebiet, at the Freiherr-vom-Stein Gymnasium in Oberhausen-Sterkrade, and took my Abitur there. Then I started studying medicine in Freiburg im Breisgau, but gave it up, just as I gave up Psychology, Philosophy and Sociology ('Don't know much about . . .') later.

However, I did manage to complete a course at the film school here in Munich, where I lived for ten years, first as a student, then as a film critic and finally as a director.

I spent the next seven years in the United States, where I finally discovered that I was German in my being and European in my profession. So I came home, and since 1984 have lived in Berlin, at the heart of the country I'm here to tell you about now.

Why tell you the story of my life? Believe me, it's not on my account, but because I'm hoping that this thoroughly German c.v. will give me licence to 'talk about Germany' and the material to do it with.

But how? I often felt like *complaining about* Germany, or being *ashamed of* Germany, I've even been known to *brag about* and to *warn* people *against* Germany. But all that's not terribly useful, you really can't go to town (to Munich now) on that. So why get up in front of a lot of people I don't know, and 'talk', seeing as I'm someone who generally does the opposite, i.e. make pictures, and who can't actually 'talk' to you, but has to read from a prepared text. Why, if not to discover something I don't yet know?

What about? About 'Germany'. The more often I say the word, the less it means to me, the more it becomes a purely geographical notion. But we're not here to talk about maps; you're all familiar with the different spaces and shapes this country has occupied in its various incarnations.

Germany. Just off the top of my head, it seems like something that no longer exists. Or that hasn't yet begun to exist again. A vacuum, if you like. Maybe not a vacuum for you, but most definitely a vacuum for me. And that's why I'm standing here: to fill that vacuum. For myself. I'm glad to have the opportunity to order my thoughts. What is 'Germany' to me? If you like, you can listen to me as I try to describe this unknown country to myself, try to give that strange word some meaning.

'Country'. The 'fatherland' or the 'mother country'. The 'big country' or the 'big wide world' . . . In fact, it's a long time since I lived in any one country. I spend more time on the road than I do at home, I travel all over the world – even, if you like, 'to the end of the world'. The world really is becoming more like a 'global village' every day. What's left for a country to be if there are no more frontiers, or if there's no difference between one side of a frontier and the other? A hopeless anachronism, especially if the country thinks of itself as a nation state, and glories in or fantasizes about that condition. We Germans ought to know that as well as anyone.

Recently Germany became 'one country' again, but are we actually 'a country' at all? And if so, which one? Exactly as before, there are two of us: one rich and one poor. One that exists in 1991, and the other in a sort of no-time, not a grey area but a grey era, so to speak, between time zones. It's always an easy way to show off to talk about jet-lag, and your body being 9 or 12 hours out of kilter. But think how it would feel if you had 9 or 12 *years* to get over.

Our xenophobia is surprising, especially when the inhabitants of the country can't define that country, don't know where it is or where their place in it is, and end up not defending their territory so much as struggling to be let into it. It seems to me we are all of us still foreigners, attempting to settle an unknown country by name of Germany. That may sound a little far-fetched, but at least it makes us all equals.

Fifteen years ago, I made a film set along the German-German border, in the remote, barely populated area at the edge of the '[Eastern] Zone'. My two shattered heroes spend the night in an American barracks, plastered with pin-ups and 'American graffiti'. They end up having a falling-out, and one of them, 'Kamikaze', leaves the place at daybreak, and the other, the 'King of the Road', wakes up alone, trudges out of the hut, and stares through the fog at the border in front of him, and the 'suicide strip'. What could he do, what gesture was open to him, when everything had been said and done? He lets out a Tarzan yell, a long, sad jungle roar. A little later, the 'King of the Road' comes to a small town, and draws up outside a cinema, where he repairs the projector, even though they've stopped showing films there. The cinema is called – it really was – 'The Blank Screen'. At that point there really was nothing left to say, and we could have ended the film right there.

When there's no 'land' in sight, can that other word 'Heimat' (home) still have any meaning? Where better to find your Heimat than when you're half a world away, in the form of 'homesickness'? I spent seven years abroad, in America. I was trying to become an American director. But I found out it wasn't enough to live 'in America', you had to live 'like an American', act and think and *speak* like an American. When I first found myself groping for a word in German that I knew in English, when I was in that awful position of stopping in mid-sentence and saying 'How do you say?', with only the English word coming to mind, I was devastated. That was when homesickness hit me. I understood I was on the point of losing something. Not just a word, and then gradually more and more words, which would have been bad enough, no, those words stood for something else, for my *language.* And by that I don't mean the language you use to express yourself, because I could express myself pretty well in the English, or rather the American, language. Rather, I mean the way language implies a certain attitude, a relationship to the world, my 'take' on it. In my language there was no 'It's nice to see you' or 'Let's have lunch some day' or 'I'll call you'. And if I said those things in America, then it wasn't *me* saying them. Halfway to becoming an American, and inevitably threatened with the loss of my German, I learned that these German words and that German grammar were a kind of scaffolding inside me, something like the extension of the spinal column into the brain. 'Ich' could never become 'I' or 'me' or 'je', not without a certain loss. And what an evocative word that is too in German – 'Ver-lust', the loss of lust, the loss of pleasure. I remember how straight after my sensation of losing German, and after years of reading only English, I read a German book, one with the wonderfully suggestive title, *Slow Homecoming* by Peter Handke, and how with each sentence my own homecoming emerged with greater clarity and urgency, back into my own language and my own world. Another factor, sure, was my disenchantment with America, but that's another story and it doesn't really belong here, OK?

Do you know where 'OK' comes from? I tried to find out all the time I was in America: 'Why do you say "OK"? KO I understand, that's short for knockout. But why "OK"?' Finally, I got an answer from a credible source. When Old Mr Ford's 'Model T' became so incredibly popular that everyone wanted one and millions of them were manufactured, the assembly line was invented and cars started being put together on a conveyor belt. The last man on the line had to give it the once-over and check it out. To begin with, he did it in longhand, but eventually with so many cars, he had to use a rubber stamp, and then he just rubber-stamped the first page of the vehicle document. Well, the man was a German, wouldn't you just know it. His name was Oskar Krause. O.K. . . . OK?

I expect Oskar Krause stayed in America. I didn't, I went back. Though *back* seems the wrong word, it felt more like going *forward*. Forward into the unknown country and the familiar language. I realized then: I live in the language, the language makes *me* live, it's a beacon of light in that so often joyless and claustrophobic country.

I was never proud of this country, I never wanted to stay in Germany. Even as a child, I only ever wanted *out*, and as soon as I was old enough to travel on my own, I got *out*, to England, to France and Spain. I now think I was not so much attracted by distant things as repelled by here. *Here*, there was the vacuum I mentioned earlier: that peculiar lack of past. You can't convince a child not to look over its shoulder. But that was the feeling I grew up with: it was wrong to look back. Behind us was a black hole, so everybody looked straight ahead for all they were worth, busied themselves with 'reconstruction', worked for the 'miracle', and that economic miracle, it seems to me now, couldn't have been achieved without a colossal effort of oblivion. The unbelievable achievement actually wasn't the phoenix: it was getting it to forget about the ashes from which it arose. A child isn't to know that, but the child I was internalized the process, and came to understand it later. Growing up in the 1950s, I experienced the German labour of repression or sublimation primarily as an absence of pleasure, of the senses, or simply, of joy. It wasn't that my parents' home was a particularly humourless or austere place, not at all; my point is that I grew up in an atmosphere that was obsessed with life as a 'serious business'. Otherwise I could never have given myself with such abandon to imported joys, such as American comic strips, American films and American music. They had one thing in common – apart from being American – they were fun, they were obvious, and they were all absolutely in the present. That sense of living for the moment and being utterly content with that was unknown to me. You can only live in the present if the past is an open book and the future beckons. That's what I learned from the American cinema. Instead of being wrapped up or half-ashamed of itself, it was 'there' and 'upfront'. No dissembling, no secrets. There was expansiveness, my own country was mean. I discovered the horizon from watching American Westerns, which, while they may have falsified American history, were still able to tell stories that were rooted in that history. I was an easy prey to those American myths, living as I was in a mythless country that liked to think it had no history and no stories. The first book I remember reading, once I learned to read, and devoured and kept re-reading, was Mark Twain's *Tom Sawyer*. It had that same sense of joy and life in the present. Huck Finn's Mississippi was more real to me than the Rhine and the Mosel.

Another example, Mickey Mouse. That merry world of pictures and stories was where I learned about life. I remember lying sick in bed once, so my mother had to go out and get the new Mickey Mouse number when she went shopping. I suppose the issue must have sold out, because my mother came back with a German strip instead. *Fix and Foxi*. You wouldn't believe how unfunny and empty and boring that seemed to me. It was the identical comic format, but so crass and so stupid, so overweeningly 'for kids', so lacking in irony, in sophistication, in jokes, that I felt real hatred for that rip-off, that imitation, that German mock-up. I'm telling you this so you can understand how desperate I was as a child to be colonized, to go to a different country than my own for instruction on such vital things as 'fun', 'laughter' and 'adventure'. The words might exist in German, but not the things they stood for.

I won't bore you with any more nostalgia for Walt Disney, especially as it's all so different nowadays anyway. Suffice it to say that I've lived out my childhood dream of the promised land, and learned that 'Entenhausen' is in fact Los Angeles, and Uncle Dagobert is Donald Trump. The dream country of my childhood has turned out to be more of a nightmare;

the fun pictures have been replaced by images of violence and a form of 'entertainment' that knocks down 'fun', 'pleasure' and 'immediacy' to the highest bidder. That sense of life that I missed so badly here as a child has become a product there, a kind of promotion. John Ford's landscapes have been renamed 'Marlboro Country', and the American Dream is an advertising campaign. That was partly why I went home, because I couldn't stand living in Disneyland any more, and because there was no longer the living breath of 'true images', only the bad breath of lies.

Back to Germany then, back to a country with its own experience of lies. It's probably the first country in recent times to be taken for a ride by lies and false images, so that, after a twelve-year dictatorship, we developed a profound distance from our own pictures and stories. I learned that twice over, once as a child from the way I was drawn to American pictures and stories, and a second time much later, when there was a renaissance of picture-making and storytelling in Germany. When we – if I may be allowed to speak for the writers and directors who made up the 'New German Cinema' – when we were ready to show our first films, we found there was no one who was ready to see them. It wasn't till long after the phenomenon of this new German film culture was blazoned abroad that a public gradually found itself for our pictures and stories from the vacuum of Germany. As ever, there is a grotesque disproportion between our images and foreign images, both on cinema screens in Germany and on German television. As ever, identification is something we import from outside, identity not produced at home, but bought in from elsewhere. I know I'm simplifying here, but I still have to say it: as ever, as much as in the post-war era, the period of the economic miracle, Germany is working and producing, exporting goods to the whole world, but we still import our images and stories, our myths, our sense of life and our dreams. And, correspondingly, the more the American economy goes into decline, the more profusely, even at times exclusively, American images engage the fantasies of the peoples of the world. Today, 10 November 1991, how many cities in the world are showing *Terminator II*, not just in one or many, but in every last one of their cinemas?

But it isn't the American cinema that I'm here to tell you about, but the vacuum in our country that sucks in foreign images and stories. The only other place I've seen which displays a similar vacuum, a similar loss of sense of self, is Japan. But I don't want to make comparisons, they're always unfair to both sides. Still, let me tell you that I once emerged from a Tokyo subway station and didn't know where I was, because there in front of me in enormous blue neon letters was the word ARBEIT. I should say that just prior to that, on the train, I had taken a picture of the people sitting opposite me, every one of them fast asleep. I was the only person in the whole carriage who was awake, and I thought to myself: They work too hard! And now, in enormous letters, the word ARBEIT. Later on, I was told that that's pretty much the only German word to be imported into Japanese: 'Arbeit-o'. The building was a publishing house that brought out a newspaper called *Arbeit-o*, a kind of advertising paper full of situations vacant, short-term work, and so on. But then I'm not here to talk to you about Japan either. I'm talking about the German vacuum. I'm talking about vacant expressions in supermarkets, in pedestrian precincts, at fast-food-outlets, in tanning studios, in video shops and sex shops, in amusement arcades and discos and on charter planes. I'm talking about armies of tourists armed with fully automatic cameras and autofocus videos, tripping through the world, never arriving anywhere, never been anywhere, until they get home and take out their holiday snaps and videos, to be able to satisfy themselves afterwards that they have actually 'been there, done that', that they have had a life. I'm talking about the German way of living at second or third or fourth hand.

It's hard enough these days to experience anything at first hand anyway. Everywhere there are the pictures, the second-hand reality. And the pictures are proliferating with breathtaking speed. Nothing can stop them, no organization, no authority. Aeons ago, and for a long time, every picture was unique. On a wall, or the wall of a cave, then on other backing like wood or canvas or the wall of a church. To see the pictures you either had to own them or else go and see them. Then there was printing, and the spread of drawings and copper etchings. Then photography. That was a great leap forward. It redefined the relationship between image, copy and reality. But because there was a negative, that meant the idea of an original still persisted, even though any number of copies could be made from it. For the first time you could see people and places without having to move. Film was a logical extension of that idea: the pictures moved, now they couldn't just describe actual things, they could invent and tell stories. Then came television, and the new idea of being able to view distant events 'live', as they happened. I remember sitting in front of a television for the first time, not at home of course, but at a friend's, whose parents didn't share the reservations of my own parents about 'the box'. More and more stations appeared, by antenna, then by cable and then satellite. At first you could see just one station, now it's ten or twenty, soon it'll be a hundred. On top of that there are videos and video cameras that allow anyone to devise their own television. Then the computers and video games, 'virtual reality' knocking on the door, and in the near future the digital image, which will finally end the distinction between original and copy, where the thousandth and millionth copy will be identical with their original, and where, quite soon, it will be impossible to check the 'veracity' of any image. In a word, images have distanced themselves more and more from reality, and have almost nothing to do with it now. Think back over the last ten or twenty years, and the expansion and inflation of images will make you quite dizzy.

Now, of course, this is happening the world over; but here, in Germany, a country that sets so much store by images and is so entirely given over to foreign images, it is perhaps at its worst. Too many images, and you lose reality. And contact with reality is just what this country, which produces so little of its own identity, needs.

I want to go back to the thing that brought me 'home' – language, the German language. As the world of images breaks all bounds, and technological advances have made images practically autonomous, to the extent that they are already practically impossible to regulate, there is another culture, an opposite culture, where nothing has changed and nothing will: the culture of words, of readings and writing and telling stories. I don't believe many things in the Bible, but I do believe, passionately, in its first sentence: 'In the beginning was the word.' I don't think it will ever say: 'At the end was the image . . .' The word will endure. Of course it's possible to wreak havoc with words too. But alongside the slogans and the political phrases and the tabloids, there will always be the writers and poets.

Nothing has substantially changed, from Homer and Plato, through Goethe and Kafka to our time. There's one person who sits down to write, and others who sit down to read. No oppression has ever been able to prevent that, no book-burning could ever break that cycle. My favourite scene in the whole of cinema is the end of Truffaut's *Fahrenheit 451*. It's a science fiction scene set in a country where books have been banned, and reading is a crime. A few outcasts live in a tented city. Every one of them is a book, has learned a book by heart and says it over and over. In a wonderful long shot at the end, you see all these 'talking books' going around, reciting in their various languages. Their Babel turns into a kind of music, a choir of mankind.

Even in this country, writing has never gone away. Unlike America, pictures are unable to forge an identity here. Not even the most moving image from German post-war politics, Willy Brandt on his knees at the memorial for the Warsaw Ghetto, had any abiding force. Images have been discredited here for once and for all. But to make up for that, we have our writing, as we have always done. There's some truth in the old adage of Germans being a people of philosophers and poets.

Our salvation [*Heil*] – some words really need to be dug out from under mounds of rubble – our salvation in this land that so badly needs some salve is our German language. It's delicate, precise, subtle, loving, sharp and careful all at once. It's rich. It's the only great wealth in a country that thinks itself wealthy, but isn't. It's everything this country no longer is, or waits to become again, or maybe never will be again.

I hope you will let someone who works in pictures say that to you. Thank you for listening.

*A talk given in the Munich Kammerspiele, 10 November 1991.*
*First published in:* Talks About Germany 2, *Munich 1991*

PART VI

# On painters, montage and dustbins
## A conversation between Wim Wenders and Jean-Luc Godard

WIM WENDERS: *I think a cigar would be appropriate.*

JEAN-LUC GODARD: Here, have one of mine.

*The last time I had a cigar was with you in San Diego. That was some time ago.*

When did we last see each other?

*I think it was at the premiere of* Detective. *After that, I think we ran into each other in a hotel lobby somewhere.*

Ah yes, the lobbies. The Jewish lobby, the Arab lobby, the hotel lobby.

*Jean-Luc, I've just seen your latest film,* Nouvelle Vague. *It looks to me as though you've become a painter. You put together your films more and more like paintings. Things have come full circle with you. Painting was around at the inception of cinema, and has often been an inspiration to directors, but usually only in individual shots. With you, though, the whole film is a painting.*

Yes. I'm toying with the idea of having my next film auctioned at Christie's, instead of putting it on in cinemas.

*That's a funny idea. Some rich American with a Godard in his safe. How are you fixed anyway: do you have your negatives, do you control your own rights?*

I never bothered much about the rights. I always sold them off for a pittance because I was short of money. And now in my old age, I'm afraid of not having enough to live on. I have to go on making films, and hope I can save a bit of money.

*I'm the opposite really. In the last three years I spent a lot of time sorting out my old films. Now I own the negatives for all of them.*

That was well done.

*Yes. It's all settled, so I don't need to think about it any more.*

Whereas a painter might be in the position of never seeing his painting again – if he's managed to sell it. Maybe he wouldn't even know where it was. I tell myself, as I love painting so much, it's only right for me to end up like a painter in that regard as well.

*Tell me something about your love of painting.*

Sometimes paintings are the only way of getting a message across – seeing them. Maybe I love paintings because it was paintings that got me interested in film in the first place. Even before I started watching films, I looked at the pictures in art and film magazines. Seeing a picture from a Murnau film, which I hadn't even seen, was what made me want to make my own films. I wanted to get involved with cinema on the strength of a printed excerpt, like a telex or something.

*For me, the discovery of cinema had a lot to do with your films, Jean-Luc. I was living in Paris at the time. When your film* Made in the USA *appeared, I went to the first screening around noon, and stayed in the cinema till midnight. It used to be that you could stay in cinemas as long as you wanted.*

Yes.

*You paid a single admission, and could see the film as many times as you wanted. I watched* Made in the USA *six times in succession.*

What a fate.

*Besides, it was winter, and it was pretty cold outside.*

Ah, now I understand.

*It was an overwhelming experience for me: I sat through the same film six times – and it was like six different films. Each time I saw something different. That's the extraordinary thing about your work. You get me to enjoy being in the role of a spectator, a child really – because that's the way you watch a film – for the pleasure of following your ideas, and at the same time coming to understand something of myself.*

Yes, it's good if a film can do that. You have to feel that it's by someone who loves his work. Without that love, it's not possible to invent anything, you dry up and it's a slow death.

*Yes, I hate it when someone feels contempt for what he does. Recently I saw a film that expressed so much contempt that I even felt despised for watching it, for being part of the audience.*

What film was that?

Angel Heart *by Alan Parker.*

I haven't seen that, but I don't much care for Alan Parker either. Even so, I don't think it's quite as you put it: Parker loves what he does all right – only he isn't very good at it. Most people love their work. Even in offices and factories things are different now: most Americans are happy with their work, if it's well paid. That's even true of soldiers: they love war. They hate the waiting, like in the Gulf now. But as soon as the first gun goes off, they'll be happy. I think even the people who did the beating in concentration camps enjoyed it. Alan Parker, or Hollywood if you'd rather, loves success.

*It was very difficult for me working in Hollywood.*

I would find it impossible.

*For instance, when I was shooting in Hollywood, I was never told how we were doing for money. So after filming for six weeks, I would have no idea whether I'd used up half the budget or just a third – or had already gone over the limit. I never knew where I was.*

That's because Americans are willing in principle to put any money into a film – as long as you give them what they want. It's just like the way they're pouring dollars into Saudi Arabia now, so long as they get the kind of war they want. I always made films where there wasn't enough money, and I couldn't raise more either. If you have ten francs, you have to try and make a film for ten francs. Rossellini taught me to respect money as a kind of artistic metaphor. Having a budget is a good discipline for creativity. If you have too much money, you just go wild, if you haven't enough, you do the opposite.

*If you have too much, it's never enough anyway.*

That's right. The important thing is using the money in a way that corresponds to my way of working. I remember how on the first day of *Breathless* we started shooting at eight o'clock in the morning and were finished by ten. We went to the cafe, and the producer came and saw us all sitting in the cafe. He was horrified and asked us, 'Why aren't you filming?' I said, 'We've finished.' Then he said, 'Well, why don't you shoot what you were going to shoot tomorrow?' And I replied, 'How do I know what we're going to shoot tomorrow?'

*Money has to be in a proper relationship to what you want to do – and the way you want to do it.*

That's what gives it its point. We're hungry, where shall we eat? How much money do we need to be able to go out and eat today? In that way, cinema's like life. If it took the manufacturers ten years to build a car, they wouldn't sell a single one. You can shoot for six or eight months, but not for four years – films that take more than a year to shoot never get finished. Pressure on time, a limited budget – that's what I mean by money as a metaphor for artistic discipline. The films I see today are all much too long anyway.

*I agree. That's really true.*

Pre-war directors still had the ability to carry a story for two hours and more. Today's directors don't have it. Most films nowadays should be an hour at the most. Books are different lengths, and paintings are different sizes, but I don't think we're any different from television really: so always the same format. The news is always the same length, whether there's a war on or not. There'd be no point to it anyway. None of us is up to making a film that lasts for an hour and a half. An hour and a half of good, dense film. I don't think the audience would tolerate it either. They can take an hour and a half of mediocrity. Then they leave thinking they're satisfied, but in fact they're disappointed.

*I'm not too good in that regard myself. My films seem to be getting longer and longer. I really admire people who are able to make eighty-minute pictures.*

The first version of my film *Breathless* went on for three and half hours. We didn't know what to do, we were at our wits' end. So we decided: we'll only keep in the bits we like. Everything else we'll cut. So in the film, if someone walked into a room, and that was followed by a scene we didn't like, we cut the scene. The man goes into a room and – cut. Or vice versa, if we didn't like him entering the room, but liked the scene in the room, then how he came to be in the damned room didn't really bother us. Whether the audience got it or not. We just kept the bits we liked.

*You are uncompromising in your fixing on the moment. You don't seem to care what comes before or after. I used not to care about chronology either. I was only interested in the moment as well. I would never have agreed that a story has to have a beginning, a middle and an end . . .*

. . . every story has a beginning, middle and end, though not necessarily in that order . . .

*. . . today I've changed my mind. I want to tell a story so it goes somewhere. One event following on another. Chronology does matter.*

I can understand that position all too well. In the 1960s we rebelled against the classical way of telling stories. We just fixed on moments. Then, when you reach a certain age, you rediscover the charm of a conventional, linear narrative. My new film, *Nouvelle Vague*, starts with the sentence: 'But I wanted to tell a story.'

*That's my problem right now. My own new film,* To the End of the World, *seems just to have gotten longer and longer. If I told it the way I wanted to, it'd be at least five hours long.*

Then have it in two parts, like *Gone with the Wind*. Or turn it into a series. I like series, even bad ones. Even *Dallas*. They have a sense of climax. We've become used to the speed of television. Television has cut the average length for a shot to two or three seconds, that's how it is in advertising. Today, I think you need to decide: if a film is going to be long, then make it really long – like six or eight hours. And if a film's short, then it should be really short – if David Lynch's new film *Wild at Heart* was ten minutes long, it would be really good. The average that everything these days comes out as is either too short or too long.

*But averageness is the prerequisite for success.*

I don't want to think like Spielberg, say. I have to say I admire him, because he doesn't make many mistakes. If he makes a film for 20,280,418 people, then you can bet between 20,280,416 and 20,280,420 will turn up to see it – you get the idea. He knows how to plan something like that. But I don't think like that. I don't like being in a room with a lot of people. I don't like being in a crowded subway car. When I go to a bakery, I don't like having to wait. So why should I want loads of people huddled in a cinema? Absolutely not: I like it when there are few people in many places. In literature, there are books with large print-runs and others with small print-runs. Samuel Beckett wrote a lot of small books that came out in tiny editions.

*We seem to be running out of patience with little things.*

And with big things too. People nowadays boast about taking six months to shoot a film. It took Tolstoy ten years to write *War and Peace*.

*When I see your films, especially the most recent ones, I'm always struck by your positioning of the camera. If you showed me a ten-second clip from* Nouvelle Vague *– I would know: that's a film by Jean-Luc.*

I choose my camera positions instinctively. Even so, I don't think the camera has been ideally placed in my films – except for the last ten or so, maybe – because there isn't any light insisting: here, this is there the camera has to stand. The camera is always there to witness the light. That's what I admire in painting: painters can create their own light.

*Can we talk about montage? Do you do your own editing?*

Yes. That's the best part of film-making. It's also the loneliest, you're all alone with your film in the cutting room. But I like that. Whereas shooting is something I don't like at all.

*. . . nor do I. I hate it . . .*

. . . I wish the crew could shoot the film without me. I think the truly creative part of making a film happens in the cutting room. I remember we had a problem with the last scene of *Nouvelle Vague*. Delon was awful in it. I tried everything, cutting it around, shortening it – suddenly I had an idea: I took out the original sound and overlaid the scene with a little sonata by Paul Hindemith. It was a great scene.

*You have a brilliant way with sound.*

I work with 24 tracks . . .

*. . . you really use 24-track sound from when you start cutting?*

Yes, if I want to.

*I'm really up against my own limitations there. I find it really difficult to envisage anything other than the original sound when I'm cutting.*

But that isn't the only possible combination. I start at the cutting table by looking at the pictures with no sound. Then I play the sound without the pictures. Only then do I try them together, the way they were recorded. Sometimes I have a feeling there's something wrong with a scene – and maybe different sound will fix it. Then I might replace a bit of dialogue with dog barks, say. Or I put in a sonata. I experiment with things until I'm happy.

*I'm shocked and impressed. I can see I'm enslaved to sound.*

It's no different than being a composer, really. He has a whole orchestra at his disposal, not just a piano. But it's still a useful discipline only to have the piano, and have to imagine the orchestra. An artistic discipline. I have the whole sound track in my head as I'm cutting. And once I've decided on the sound, I cut the scene, and throw the rest in the bin.

*In the bin? Are you so sure of yourself, do you never go back and change anything afterwards?*

Well, maybe there's the odd occasion I run to the bin before the binmen get there the next morning. But it hardly ever happens.

*First appeared in:* Süddeutsche Zeitung Magazin, *16 November 1990*

## 'I'm at home nowhere'
### Acceptance speech for the Murnau Prize

Friedrich-Wilhelm Murnau was a great innovative storyteller and pictorial artist of the cinema, one of the few genuine landmarks of the seventh art. He was far ahead of his time, too far perhaps to be able to bridge that gulf for long. He lived like someone born in the latter part of this century, not the last.

It's a great honour to receive a prize bearing his name. It's a great honour to follow in the footsteps of Eric Rohmer, the first recipient of the Murnau Prize. I'd like to thank the Murnau Society, the town of Bielefeld and the Bielefeld Banking Association for giving me this honour.

Many things in cinema have changed since the time Murnau made his films in Germany and America. The whole world has changed. And if it's not quite true to say that it's cinema that has changed the world, it is at least partly true. Storytelling has changed, images have changed, the transmitting and receiving of images has changed, our sense of the world has changed, to such a degree that Friedrich-Wilhelm Murnau would be quite dizzy, if he were to be exposed to the profusion and variety of images and the type of image language that we're used to seeing every day of our lives – especially the tenderest among us, our children.

It's a turbulent time for the cinema.

So it seemed appropriate to choose for this evening's screening, a film that tries to draw up a kind of balance sheet of the cinema, exactly fifty years after Murnau's death. It's no accident that it's in black and white, or that the director character in the film goes by the name of Friedrich Munro. Nor is it a coincidence that the film begins in Europe, at the most westerly point of Portugal, where Europe sticks its nose out to America, or that it ends with the death of the director on a street that's barely an hour's drive from where Murnau died. The night before his death, Friedrich, our director, stands in a phone box, and quotes a diary entry of Friedrich-Wilhelm Murnau's: 'I'm at home nowhere, in no house, in no country . . .' Maybe the film, *The State of Things*, was a little too dark, from its depressed perspective. Ten years have passed since then, and 'the state of things' is different again.

The cinema is facing a change as drastic and comprehensive as the quantum leap from silent to sound film. The age of photography and the photographic image – and hence of cinema – is approaching its end. At the end of this era, as it enters the new era of digital electronic images, perhaps the cinema will be able to summon up all its strength, and do what it was intended for: to show twentieth-century people their image, in reality as in dream. Friedrich-Wilhelm Murnau would be a great inspiration for such a feat. Surely, he would also be the first to warn us today against sentimentalizing the old cinema, and against being too gloomy about the coming age of digital image recording. He was a pioneer. He would be one if he were with us today. Pioneers are optimists by nature, and that's why they tell you more about the future than the past.

My own view of the future of cinema is less bleak than it was in 1981, when I made *The State of Things*. New perspectives have opened up that were less evident then, or perhaps some of my old bogeymen have disappeared. There is no longer the arch-enemy 'television' and the devil 'video', because behind and beyond them there is a possible new ally and a new cinematic language in the form of the high resolution digitally sorted image which is currently being developed. Nor is there any more the 'wicked' and overweening American film industry, and the 'poor' little national producers in Germany, France, Italy, Spain, England, Poland, Scandinavia, USSR, etc. There is a growing sense of a 'European cinema' as a proud language common to all these countries, and, one hopes, not just a language, but a functioning European institution and industry, a protective roof that will assure the small national industries of their survival. (And for how much longer? No one knows. Let's say: for as long as possible, as long as cinema in some form still exists.)

Because such a roof demands solid beams and supports, I would like to suggest that Friedrich-Wilhelm Plumpe, better known as Murnau, native of Bielefeld, be taken less as a pioneer of the German cinema, than as one of the great forerunners of our common European cinema.

Thank you very much for listening.

*Bielefeld, 17 March 1991. First appearance*

## King of Comedy
Contribution to a discussion in the 'Probebetrieb Filmwerkstatt',
Arsenal, Berlin

Please excuse my absence. Because of unforeseeable and sudden family obligations that sadly demand my presence, I am not able to be in Berlin this evening. Still, it seems in keeping with the title of the evening, 'Experimental Film Workshop' that someone like Hanns Zischler is prepared to stand in for me.

I wanted to watch Martin Scorsese's film *King of Comedy* with you, and discuss it with you afterwards. I wasn't going to deliver a lecture or give you my opinion, rather I would have liked to point out a few features of the film *in advance*, and discuss them with you afterwards.

I didn't choose *King of Comedy* because, as it rather misleadingly says in the programme notes, 'it has influenced my own work', but rather because I think it is the most important and most misunderstood American film in the last ten years; it's shown far too rarely, and because the scathing reception it got from the American media (resulting in the film's failure at the box office) made me hopping mad. What this film offers is a radical critique of the American concept of *entertainment*. I would have liked to talk about that concept with you after seeing the film. You should know that in America it's an industry of roughly the same size as the automobile industry, if you look at the whole thing from production and distribution through to the cinema chains as a single entity. That colossus is covered by the seemingly harmless term 'entertainment', which barely translates into the sweet German word 'Unterhaltung'. An 'entertainer' wouldn't become president in Germany, but in the USA one did. 'Entertainment' in the USA is nothing less than an imperative.

It seems that an American film may only criticize this system if it plays by the rules of 'entertainment' itself.

The film *Broadcast News* recently did just that, in quite intelligent fashion. *King of Comedy* is altogether more *radical*, because it won't play by the rules. Quite the contrary. Having cast a household name from the American entertainment industry (Jerry Lewis) and thereby seeming to promise entertainment, the film instead proceeds to deliver a pitiless analysis of that craving as a 'late capitalist' structure, interested only in money, and exposes 'show business' for the cynical and contemptuous sham it is, with the 'show' on the outside, and nothing but 'business' at its heart. The unique and radical thing about Scorsese's film is that it does all that, while steadfastly refusing to become a 'show' itself. Instead of delivering 'a good show', which it certainly has the plot to do, it is set on seeing.

On unmasking.

The way Scorsese avoids having to play by the rules and entertain, especially with the Jerry Lewis character, and how the hero, the De Niro character, never lives up to that expectation either, but keeps deflecting and reflecting it instead is quite breathtaking. The American reviewers were so incensed by Scorsese's film that they were frothing at the mouth, which in turn exposed their job as little better than pimping for the industry. With *King of Comedy*, Scorsese puts a question mark against American film criticism just as much as the entertainment industry it was meant to be criticizing.

This is an uncompromising film. In the way that most 'anti-war' films end up by being pro-war, by lionizing it or being unable to resist its glamour (*Platoon* is a recent example of this), i.e. that films can never really distance themselves from what they mean to be critical of (because the mere fact of portrayal brings in the viewer's sympathies), so films about Hollywood or 'America' have generally ended up as positive in spite of themselves. Not *King of Comedy*.

It's one of the rare films that are genuinely critical of America. Its criticism is aimed at the most vulnerable point of the American psyche, the basis of American *culture*, which is an entertainment culture. It's practically a treasonable film. It deals with the entertainment industry as if it were the arms industry. Which it is. American television, the subject of the film, is the arms industry that aims inside people's heads.

I should have liked to discuss all this with you after the film. A song comes to mind : 'Hanns can do it.' Maybe he'll conduct such a discussion with you.

And if not, at least you will have had an opportunity of seeing the film in the original version.

*1988. First appearance*

## Christ, Rainer

Christ, Rainer,
when did I first see you?

I think it was in the 'Bungalow', that bar in the Türkenstrasse in Schwabing. There were a couple of pinball machines in the back room. In the front room was a jukebox. A few film posters on the walls, wooden benches, wooden chairs, wooden tables, with graffiti etched into them. The 'Bungalow' was a fairly minimal hangout.

I remember: there was a girl dancing alone in front of the jukebox, in a mini-skirt, curly hair pinned up. That was Hanna. And the guy who stood around and watched her for hours, holding a beerglass, that was you. There were some other people, and the whole gang of you were involved with theatre in some way. Then there was our gang, the 'Munich softies', students at the film school, directors like Klaus Lemke, Rudolf Thome and Martin Müller, and a few people who wrote for a tiny journal called *Filmkritik*.

One day we heard Rainer had made a film with Hanna in it, in very quick time and with next to no money. That was *Katzelmacher*. That was when we started to look at you in a different way, even though aesthetically you had nothing in common with us softies. But we had to take our hats off to you! You'd made a film! Something most of us only dreamed of doing, in those days.

Then I remember several years in which we used to see each other at the 'Filmverlag der Autoren', working laboriously but with real solidarity on getting a film production and distribution company going, along with fifteen other directors. That was the nucleus of the 'New German Cinema', a purely practical and financial organization. Unlike the directors of the French New Wave, say, we had no aesthetic or cultural programme, and in all the years we saw each other and spoke regularly, there was never a word about the content or style of films.

Once, years later, we ran into each other in Hollywood, at an Oscar ceremony. I have no idea what we were doing there. Anyway, we stood in a corridor, feeling pretty out of it in our dinner jackets, and there, thousands of miles away from home, we first asked each other about work.

I can remember another meeting, late at night in the museum cinema in Munich. You wanted to show your new film to a handful of friends and associates. You'd just finished it, and were very proud of it. We watched your working copy with the just-completed mix of *The Marriage of Maria Braun*. The film was unusually carefully made by your standards, and it was obvious that you had stayed with it right to the end. I say that because in some of your films it's clear that you didn't, that while they were in the final stages of editing, you were already elsewhere, onto the next film. This one carried your signature right the way through. Out in the rain, after the film, with the little group of us standing around and congratulating you, there was a stunned feeling and a sense that the 'New German Film' was, all at once and just for a moment, a conspiratorial entity, and our solidarity was more than just the means to an end.

The last time I met you was during the Cannes Film Festival in May 1982. I had asked a whole lot of directors to come up to a room in the hotel where we'd set up a camera and a Nagra, for them all to say a few words about the future of cinema, alone with the equipment. You were standing by the bar of the Hotel Martinez in the late morning, looking frighteningly washed-up, pale and dog-tired. I told you about my project and the question and you went up to the room. What you said and did in front of the camera I only saw a couple of days later. And then, a couple of months after that, when I got around to editing *Chambre 666*, you were already dead.

I remember: I had arrived in Munich on the night train, stepped out onto the station forecourt in bright sunshine, and blinking my eyes, caught the headlines on the newspaper stands, all with the same import. Rainer Werner Fassbinder is dead. Strange though it may sound, it seemed to me we should all have realized for some time that that had always been your destination.

It's now ten years that you've been dead, and we all live with your loss, which isn't getting any smaller; on the contrary, we also miss the films you would have made in that time.

So long.

*Written in Berlin, 6 March 1992 for the catalogue for the retrospective on the tenth anniversary of Rainer Werner Fassbinder's death*

PART VII

# On making it up as you go along
## Conversation with Friedrich Frey

FRIEDRICH FREY: *You like to quote in your films; a scene of yours will refer to a scene in some older film. In* Wings of Desire, *your latest, there are some striking examples. But it looks to me as though when you quote now, you do it in a different way. Your allusion to Nicholas Ray in* Kings of the Road *is very different to your quoting Chaplin's* The Circus *in your new film. What does it mean to you, anchoring yourself in cinema history – and has your practice of it changed at all?*

WIM WENDERS: 'Dropping anchor' in that way was much more important to me in my early films. Something like *The Goalkeeper's Fear of the Penalty* is one big anchor. Almost every shot in that film is a reference to Hitchcock. I think you do that compulsively, almost unconsciously in your first films. You're entering a landscape that a lot of previous explorers have been through and left their traces in, and you use a language and a grammar that others have used before you, in order to tell a similar kind of story. Because there isn't an unlimited supply of stories or myths. You keep running into things that other people have done before you, things that they already found a language and a form for. It's inevitable. Probably the most comprehensive and conscious quote is the one you mentioned, in *Kings of the Road*: 'Coming home, to the place of your childhood.' When I was on location on that island in the Rhine near Bacharach, trying out various ways of doing that coming-home-to-the-place-of-your-childhood with the actor Rüdiger Vogler, that scene from Nicholas Ray's *The Lusty Men* that has Robert Mitchum coming home, and crawling under the house to get that tin box with his childhood treasures out of its old hiding place – that seemed so much the essence of what we wanted to say, and so unimprovable as the right form for our scene, that we ended up quoting it – or doing a variation on it, more like. In *The American Friend* there aren't any whole quoted scenes like that, but a lot of other references to the prehistory of cinema, in the form of all those gadgets like the zoetropes, the wooden Maltese cross, or the lamp next to the little boy's bed with the steam train rushing through the landscape. The whole of *The State of Things* was a film about film-making, and it begins with a homage to a film from the 50s, *The Most Dangerous Man Alive* by Alan Dwan, who was well over 80 at the time, alive as a cricket, and who once told me in Hollywood about that time when he already had twenty or thirty films under his belt, and this young director by the name of Griffith came along, and did everything differently and made film-making terribly complicated. I met Alan Dwan in the late 1970s. It was amazing, talking to someone who'd seen the whole history of cinema unfold, right from the very beginning!

The time of quoting, and my need and my wanting to refer to the history of cinema, ended with *The State of Things*. I had put in question narrative, the grammar and the morality of film-language, but the contention of the director in the film (and mine too, for that matter), that 'stories only exist in stories', had been disproved by the film itself. So I was in the mood for unconditional, unfettered narrative, that didn't need to prove itself or advertise itself. So all forms of quoting were out of the question, unnecessary, a no-no. *Paris, Texas* was a film without any references, at least there isn't any glaring example to the contrary, not so far as I know. Which isn't to say that people can't go hunting for quotes or traces of earlier films in it, of course. The quotation from Charlie Chaplin's film that you mentioned in relation to *Wings of Desire* is a bit like that. I wasn't at all aware of it during the shot, it was only when we looked at the proofs that Solveig Dommartin pointed out to me that the scene with her sitting alone on a round patch of sawdust is an unmistakeable echo of the last shot in *The Circus*. That kind of thing just arises from the scene and the subject-matter: when you take down a circus tent, you're left with this ring of sawdust. And if a member of the troupe stays behind while the rest of them move on, it seems almost inevitable that they would be standing in that ring of sawdust and be waving to the others. And there's your 'quote', which just pops up like a genie.

*You mean it wasn't a conscious borrowing at all?*

Absolutely not. But of course I could see it right away, and I had to laugh, because the similarity was quite striking. Maybe there's another, more general type of quoting going on in *Wings of Desire* on the level of light. Because we had Henri Alékan as our cameraman, and his outstanding black and white cinematography may have given the film something of the quality of French films from the 1940s and 50s. And that period, when poets like Cocteau and Prévert were working in the French cinema, may have inspired us in a general way to approach our film in a poetic way, and give it something of the form of a poem. That was what Peter Handke and I had in mind anyway, and we were emboldened by films like *Les Visiteurs du Soir* and *Les Enfants du Paradis*. We didn't 'quote' from those films at all, but it's possible we had something of the same attitude or the same 'take' in the way we wanted to tell our story.

But I think your question is more to do with how in your own work you come to – you want to – echo some previous work. I think it's different in cinema from how it is in literature or painting or music. There's only a limited list of stories, scenes, situations that keep recurring in all kinds of variations. Maybe it's to do with the concreteness of film images, or maybe that our own lives repeat the same situations over and over, and film is closer to 'life' than the other arts. But whatever: because a film is practically forced to repeat the same situations and scenes anyway, I think it's only right to acknowledge that similar things have been said before, instead of claiming to have come up with something brand new. It's more scrupulous to say: 'I'm telling you this thing here, but it's been shown before in such and such a place.' It's better to let on that you know something, than to claim it's entirely yours.

*So no 'genius aesthetic' for you?*

Of course not! I find it really salutary to feel I'm in a kind of family, to be working into a family of images. Originality isn't that important or that much worth pursing in the cinema. On the contrary: I'm pleased and relieved to be working in a language and with a film grammar that seem positively classical to me. Maybe it's to do with getting older. I tend to be less and less impressed when somebody 'invents' something (I'm talking about storytelling now), because it's mostly hype, and generally happens at the expense of the actual story. I think the cinema came up with the idea of storytelling at a certain point in its development, and there's not all that much you can do to improve on it. Where you can make an improvement, and where you should do your darnedest to invent, or to find something new, is the kind of story you tell: not so much *how* you tell it, as *what* you tell. I'm really not that bothered with finessing around with film language, and making something more aesthetic or 'genial'. But I will always try to say something useful – and I hope, with luck, something new – in that classical language, which I hold in the highest regard. To me film history is a very peaceful kind of place, where it's worth dropping anchor. It's a good place to be, and you're in good company.

*To return to* Wings of Desire. *Something I wanted to ask from when I first saw it: the look of your angels. How did you come to have your angels as they are?*

That was a pretty chaotic process. When we started shooting, we had no idea how the angels should look. And so the first three days we filmed without them, or we left out the countershots of the two of them. We were filming everything in chronological order, so we had the children staring up at the sky or into the camera, when they're seeing the angels. And in between, we kept running tests with Bruno Ganz and Otto Sander, putting them in different costumes every half hour, all this armour and white robes, with various wigs and all kinds of different make-up. It was pretty ridiculous. The two of them were there, they were there in the shooting schedule, but still we couldn't film them, because we couldn't decide on how they ought to look. I suppose it was quite a far-reaching decision to have to make. Then at the end of the third day of filming, I said: 'All right, I've had enough of all that stuff with angels' robes and suits of armour, just stick them in coats.' So on the fourth day of the shoot by now, the wardrobe-mistress set off with them, and they bought coats, just ordinary coats. The only thing left of all the amazing wigs and hairstyles were their little ponytails, that was the last trace of all our costume ideas, and it was pretty funny at the start: Otto came on set, in pancake make-up in a white coat, with a bit of armour peeking out underneath (the armour puts in a brief appearance in the film), and the children were completely appalled and said: 'What, do you think angels look like that?' And secretly that was what we all thought too.

*It can't do much for your nerves, if you're starting shooting, and you don't know what your main characters are going to look like!*

It was a critical thing, and our nerves were pretty much twanging. It was frustrating for the main actors too; we were starting the film, and they didn't even know what they were going to wear. We had so little idea about 'angels'. The more we talked, the less we knew. So I finally decided just to start the film, unprepared. I thought I would lose the film and the poetry of the idea if I knew too much, or was even sufficiently 'prepared'. And all the medieval debates we got into! Such as does an angel's hair move in the wind? Seeing as they are spiritual creatures, the wind should pass through them. Then how do we get their hair to be so stiff that it doesn't blow around, but still looks like hair? Or does an angel get wet in the rain? My God, all the things we were worried about! But they all vanished once we got going.

*And you weren't worried at all?*

Oh, of course we were. But much more worried by the idea of the whole thing being thought through into the tiniest detail, and all styled to death. I told the actors, the cameraman and the art-director that we would only be able to reach or maintain the level of poetry in the film if we worked like poets ourselves, which is to say spontaneously. If the film had been storyboarded and everything planned out in advance, it could never have turned into a poem.

*I'm reminded of your description of the way you worked on* Kings of the Road, *when you filmed one day without knowing what you'd do the next. Did you go back to that method in* Wings of Desire, *or is it more something you've always done?*

One way or another, it's something I've done pretty often. *Kings of the Road* was an extreme case, I suppose, because the only script we had for that was our road map. *The State of Things* came about in a similar way, with the difference being that we had two locations, but they were an awfully long way apart: the coast of Portugal and Hollywood. *Nick's Movie* had no screenplay either of course, and less 'story' than the others too. But of course it was also a bigger and more compelling story than any invention, because it was the life of Nicholas Ray, and we were in the hands of a 'director', Death, who couldn't care less whether the camera was loaded or people knew their lines or anything else. *Paris, Texas* was kind of a mixture. The first half of it was all written and planned, and the second was an empty page. For *Wings of Desire* we had a few fixed points, a few 'lighthouses' in the form of the four great dialogues that Peter Handke had written for it. Apart from that, the action and most of the scenes were devised during the actual shoot. Every night I got together with Clare, my assistant, and with Richard Reitinger, and we wrote the scenes for the next day – or the day after, if things were going particularly well. But as I say, we had the scenes Peter had given us, that we could row towards in the dark, and from each of those lighthouses we could see the next one winking to us in the distance . . .

*Then how did you get the idea of having the TV-Columbo, Peter Falk, in* Wings of Desire? *He represents some kind of anchor too, doesn't he?*

We had that idea in our very first treatment. There was going to be this big American film being shot, although that in itself wasn't really important, and there was going to be this figure in it who would turn out to be a former angel, and was now a famous actor. By the time we started filming, we'd rejected that idea, only to come round to it again two or three weeks in. For me the idea had a kind of lightness to it, and I didn't want it to get entirely lost in the film. At the beginning I was thinking of the whole thing in terms of a comedy anyhow, with these unemployed angels and so on. But after a couple of weeks of shooting, we realized the idea was too poetic to be used just for laughs, and we began to take the idea of the angels very seriously, and I wanted it to be taken seriously, although always with the possibility of the whole thing tipping over the edge (and in some scenes I think it does).

So it seemed to me we were short of that kind of levity or grace, and so I went back to the idea of the former angel. And that angel would have to be played by someone incredibly well-known. There were all sorts of other ideas floating around too, but they went by the board. The last thing we were left with was that it would have to be a movie actor, because they are really the most familiar faces. After that we proceeded quite systematically. What actors are really well known all over the world?

Well, they would have to be American, and would also have to have done a lot of television work. And so we went through the list of actors who are known for film and telly, looking for someone of exceptional 'human' warmth – that was the character – and finally there was no other possibility.

And I said all that to Peter Falk, I called him up and told him we're making a film, we're in the third week of the shoot, and I didn't have anything in writing that I could show him. The idea is: former angel; and then there are these other out-of-work angels. But you've been a human being for some time, and you tell them: 'Hey, this is all right, why don't you come on down!' That, in a nutshell, is what I said to Peter Falk on the phone, and of course I was pretty excited with it. It's not every day you get to talk to Columbo on the phone! At first he was quite stunned, and then after a longish pause, he asked me how I'd thought of him. 'By deduction,' I said. He'd been rumbled as a former angel. He laughed, and a couple of days later he said he was in. I think not least because there was nothing for him, not even a single page to look at.

*But Peter Falk actually has a very detailed characterization in the film, what with his grandmother and everything. Is that straight out of Peter Falk's life?*

Yes, that was his own contribution. His inner monologue, the voiceover, we had to do afterwards – we had him just for the one week he was able to be over here. So he was back in LA and couldn't get away, and I couldn't fly over to record it with him. So we discussed everything on the telephone, and he recorded it by himself in a studio. I'd sent him some material for the voiceover, and he used some of it; but from time to time he also shut his eyes, and just said whatever came into his head. Almost all of what finished up in the film were his own things. He kept coming back to his grandmother, that was one of them. Of course that was completely wrong, because if you're an angel, you're hardly going to have a grandmother, but what the heck.

*First appeared in:* Frankfurter Rundschau, *10 September 1988*

## Writing a screenplay is the worst
Conversation with Rainer Nolden

RAINER NOLDEN: *You have just been awarded the Ministry of the Interior's Gold Ribbon for Film for your latest production,* Wings of Desire. *In Rotterdam you were selected as 'Most Promising Director for the Future', and you were awarded the Bavarian Film Prize for showing the way forward to a new, sensitive, original type of cinema. How do you see this renewal happening?*

WIM WENDERS: That's up to the critics, I would say, it's not really for me to interpret myself. For what it's worth, I have the feeling that *Wings of Desire* was quite an imaginative piece of work, and told an unusual kind of story. It's to do with many things that people are familiar with from their childhood, the images that a whole generation – my own – has of Germany. Its innovativeness lies in the way the story's told, where both the look and the sound of the film play a role. The camera is the eye of the invisible angel – which makes it very mobile and flexible. At the same time, the eye of the angel is full of affection for mankind. And because angels can also hear people's thoughts, the sound of the film is very complex as well.

*But couldn't it equally have been the sky over New York or Düsseldorf?* *

Absolutely not, Berlin was the original inspiration for the film. Before we had the idea of the guardian angels, before we had any kind of plot, I wanted to make a film about Berlin. The idea came out of the complexity of the city, if you like, and the attempt to find a way of storytelling that could accommodate a lot of different 'angles'. The angels are a device that enables me to talk about Berlin. No other place would have given me that idea. The whole atmosphere of the film, the fact of it being in black and white . . . in Frankfurt or Hamburg or Düsseldorf, I would never have thoughts of making a film in black and white.

*A reference to the original title, Der Himmel über Berlin (The Sky over Berlin) (Trans.).

*You learned your craft at the film school in Munich. But is directing a profession that can be learned, or are such establishments only conduits to channel already existing talents along – one hopes – the right lines?*

I had already made a few shorts by that time. But they were pretty much the films of a painter who was trying to paint with a camera instead of canvas and oils. The first film in which I told a story, in which I was a director, and not just a painter behind a camera, was done in film school; it was called *Alabama – 2000 Light Years*. Directing was something I invented for myself, the way Fassbinder and Herzog did too. I think the only one of us who was really taught was Volker Schlöndorff; he was Louis Malle's assistant, among other things. But the majority of the people involved with the New German Cinema were self-taught. Where I actually learned the most was being a film reviewer for four or five years.

*Between 1978 and 1984 you were out of the country. Did you find that conditions for film-makers had changed much in that period?*

Yes, I think they did. When I left in 1978, there was still some of the euphoria of the early 70s around. There was a spirit of adventure, which was behind a lot of those films. The whole of Fassbinder's output was certainly highly adventurous, and people like Günter Rohrbach, who was the head of television drama at the WDR [Westdeutscher Rundfunk], really went out on a limb when he backed those films. But seven years later, after my stay in the USA, I felt the atmosphere in Germany had changed. There was an emphasis on playing safe, even a kind of self-censorship that people practised towards institutions. People were forever saying, 'That's not commercial enough, that's too daring, too different, too outrageous . . .' Or they would say, 'We can't do that, they'd never touch it.' Projects were weighed up even before they were submitted to television or the film finance bodies. So a lot had changed in seven years. Not much of that 70s adventurousness was left. A cold bureaucratic wind was blowing everywhere.

*Alfred Hitchcock said script-writing was his favourite part of film-making: the shooting was almost a chore he had to do afterwards. What part of making a film is most important for you?*

Writing is the worst. I hate that like the plague. What I really like doing are the practical preparations: travelling around and looking for locations and people, trying to find my film, not by writing it, but by a kind of pre-cognition. After that, I like editing an awful lot. Shooting – I've yet to meet the director who says he enjoys it. It can be great sometimes, but it's also a real slog. François Truffaut once said that after three or four weeks of shooting, the only thing he cared about was the thing being finished – and himself still alive at the end of it.

*Isn't part of that the fear of one's own work being taken away from one by one's collaborators?*

Not by my collaborators, on the contrary. The only person I ever think is going to lose my film is me. Especially because pretty much all my films, with the exception of *Hammett*, were done with, shall we say, a rather open screenplay. I've always changed things around a lot, sometimes I made up the story as we went along, like on *Kings of the Road* and *The State of Things* and *Nick's Movie*. So what I tend to be afraid of is me losing control of a thing, rather than other people taking it away from me.

*Do you think films, in particular your own films, can have any effect? The stories they tell are very personal. I could imagine most people wouldn't have much in common with your characters.*

That's not how I see it. I would never go around saying 'I know my audience', but I do know plenty of people who have seen my films, and who may be representative, I don't know. After every film I make, I spend months travelling around with it, showing it to people and talking to them afterwards. In that way I am in contact with my audience.

*But the films were already finished by that time, you're not talking about previews in the American sense.*

Oh, I don't care for that at all: showing a film before it's finished. I only did that once – had to do it – and that was for *Hammett*, and it was a dreadful experience. It felt like I was having to sell myself, saying: 'Do you like this? Never mind, then, I'll change it!'

*Some of your films are already established as cult movies. I'm thinking of*

Alice in the Cities, *which has a particular set of fans, or* Kings of the Road. *What makes a cult-film?*

The connection between a cult-film and its audience. The film gives it audience more than films usually do: they satisfy a need in the audience not in a quasi-industrial way, but in a personal, intimate way.

*But that has to be down to chance. You don't walk into a studio and say: 'Now we're going to make a cult-film.'*

It *has* to be by chance. Anything else would be cynical. A cult-film, by definition, is a film that has found an audience – not one that was *made* for an audience.

*What would be a 'typical' cult-film for you?*

I can think of a few: films I'm always ready to see any time. For instance *Salt of the Earth* by Herbert J. Biberman, Hawks's *Only Angels have Wings*, Bob Rafelson's *Five Easy Pieces* or Jim Jarmusch's *Stranger than Paradise*.

*You've said that not feeling at home is good for a film-maker. That feeling comes up a lot in your films. Is it fair to conclude that you're a fairly rootless character yourself?*

I suppose so, although it isn't so much a trait of my own films, as much as something that's present in the medium as a whole. 'Motion pictures' is what they're called, after all. That motion is something highly symbolic for me. There's a whole school of films that deal with not feeling at home. Film is an invention of our century, which makes it the ideal medium for our own time, and lack of roots and lack of home are big contemporary themes.

*Which of your films would you say was your most personal?*

*Nick's Movie*, the film I made with Nicholas Ray. But that's personal in such an extreme way that it doesn't really come into the category of your question. I think it would be a difficult choice between *Wings of Desire* and *Alice in the Cities*.

*Nick's Movie is a very intimate film. I could imagine you almost felt hesitant about recording a person dying.*

Not almost hesitation. Every day, with every shot, we asked ourselves: 'Can we do this?' The whole film was accompanied by these ethical, moral dilemmas. And I think it shows. And then every day – almost in spite of us – we felt we had to carry on, for Nick's sake.

*What does it feel like training your camera on a dying man?*

Awful. And I wouldn't have done it either, if the dying man hadn't needed it – as a task, as therapy, as an act of friendship. It was like that for the whole crew.

*Is there a point when you're working when you relax, feel comfortable, and say: 'This is my film'?*

That varies from film to film. With *Wings of Desire* I thought up until the very last day of it, 'What is this you've let yourself in for?' While some other films have given me a feeling of security from the start, you just know it'll 'pan out'. Other films give you weeks of sleeplessness and anxiety and doubts and fears. Others again 'sweep you away'. On *Paris, Texas* I had that sense of something happening: with us, behind the camera, with the actors in front of it, and with Sam Shepard's script – it was all bigger than I'd ever thought possible. We were all caught up in the film, it was like a boat that I had to steer. The story swept us away like a great river.

*Are there any films you don't like at all?*

Horror films. To me it's an absurd idea, making films in order to frighten people. Films are there to take away fear, and create peace and serenity.

*But evidently there is public demand for such frightening films.*

Oh sure. Only I want no part of it.

*Couldn't they also take away fear too, have some therapeutic function? You want to achieve something with the films you make, why should it be any different for Brian de Palma, say?*

Don't tell me his horror films are really therapeutic in intention. I just don't believe that. I don't believe people make horror films for any other reason than making money.

*But don't you want to do that with your films too? Surely it's a legitimate aspiration, isn't it?*

Yes, it's a legitimate aspiration. A painter can say, in the same way, that it's his legitimate aspiration to get rich from his painting. And I don't have a problem with painters getting rich from their paintings; I'm glad that Joseph Beuys, say, got a lot of money for his stuff. But at the same time that's not why he created it. Of course, films are a bit different, because you need a lot of money to make a film at all. And that being so, the aspiration to earn money for your films is completely legitimate, because that's the only way you'll be able to make another one. That's why I produced all my own films. I'm one of not that many directors in the world who own the rights to their own films – except for *Hammett* – and are in a position to decide what happens to them. As for earning money, in the end I put everything I made from my films – when I did make anything – into the next one. It was never that much anyway, except with *Paris, Texas,* – although over time my old films will make money too.

*So it's not making you rich?*

It's a living. I didn't get rich, because I plough it all back into the next one – and hence into remaining independent. Well, in a sense, I am rich. The fact that I own these fourteen films, that's a kind of life insurance in the long run.

*Would you be able to express yourself in a different medium – painting, say?*

Certainly. I like writing too.

*But didn't you just say writing was the worst?*

Yes, writing a screenplay is the worst. But writing a story is a nice thing to do. Writing for a film, sitting at a typewriter to come up with a film, and then having to make it afterwards – that's torture.

*How would you distinguish German cinema from other European cinema, or from American cinema? What characterizes a German film?*

The German film has an introverted character, it likes to ponder existential questions. Or maybe that's just a cliché, because there are German action films and German comedies too. I do think there's a kind of inwardness that's typical of German cinema, though, just as it's typical of German literature and German art as well. And hell, that can be a good thing. One shouldn't always pretend it's a terrible fault of German films.

*You've directed one stage production, Peter Handke's* Round the Houses. *Would you like to do more work for the stage?*

Yes, I would like to, although it's not an easy matter, switching from being a film-maker to a theatre director. They are two completely different things; I learned that from my experience. There are far better theatre directors than I'll ever be. I think I did a decent job with Peter's play, because my approach was terribly naive. It was like a single-shot film on stage.

*A three-hour-long shot!*

Of course you need to rethink, to learn to see the actors as the essential thing. That's the peculiar thing about theatre: you can do all kinds of things in rehearsal, and when it's the première and you're sitting in the stalls, you see a different film from the one you made. It's like a 'living film'. I learned a lot, especially humility from the actors I was used to bossing around in films, because there it's the director who's the lord over the images, and what the actors do is only visible if it's on camera. Theatre is quite different, and it was a good and valuable experience for me.

*You say, 'bossing around', but you're hardly the dictatorial type of director, are you?*

I meant 'boss around' in the sense of being the only person with 'the big picture', with an overall sense of what's going on in my head. Most of the time actors don't know. Especially if they're playing small parts; coming in to a shoot for two or three days, they really can have no idea of the sort of film they're appearing in. Still less if someone shoots in chronological sequence, the way I do. Someone comes along, and you don't have the time to do a whole lot of talking, you just try and tell them about the particular situation they appear in. The actor's really at your mercy.

*Practically all your films are stories about men. Are you not interested in women's stories?*

I've done a couple.

*But without much conviction.*

At the time, I wanted *The Scarlet Letter* to tell the story of a woman. In a way, I felt I didn't really have the right to tell the story of a woman, because I could only make assertions based on my own experience. It's very important to me to make films based on my own experience. When women started making films in the 1970s based on *their* experience and about *them*selves, I was full of admiration, and it seemed quite logical to me for a man to make films about men – but not in the way films have traditionally done that. I mean, I suppose 80 per cent of all films were to do with men anyway. The whole tradition of the Western is a men thing. But I really thought: if it's OK for women to go out and start investigating their identity as women, and defining themselves as women, then why not have a genre of men's films that define men.

*You're about to set off round the word with a new project. What is it exactly?*

A science fiction film called *To the End of the World.*

*Something that's been on your mind for some time . . .*

Yes, I started writing it in 1977/8 when I was in South East Asia, and then in Australia. Then I got the fabled telegram from Hollywood, and I decided to make *Hammett* first. I was going to spend a year on that, and then go back to Australia to shoot my science fiction story. But instead there was a delay of several years. Now I'm picking up the thread again, inevitably in a slightly different form, although the basic idea is still the same.

*What is* To the End of the World *about?*

It's a love story that plays over three years, finishing in the year 2000. It's the story of a woman.

*So you are making a woman's story after all . . .*

*First appeared in:* Die Welt, *20 June 1988*

# On walls and spaces
## Conversation with Jochen Brunow

JOCHEN BRUNOW: *Your films are often based on literary models, although it would be wrong to call them book adaptations. If we leave out* Summer in the City *as your graduation film at film school, then your very first feature film was based on a book. Do you have particularly strong literary leanings. How did this come about?*

WIM WENDERS: Peter Handke and I were already friends at the time. When Peter showed me the manuscript of *The Goalkeeper's Fear of the Penalty,* before the book came out, I thought: this reads just like a film; every sentence is like a shot. Then, when we talked about it, Peter said half-jokingly, then why don't you make a film of it!

*How was it to adapt? Did you make a regular screenplay to shoot from?*

Well, I had to write a screenplay to finance the film, because I was completely unknown. I didn't want to show the WDR (Westdeutscher Rundfunk) *Summer in the City* either, because I thought the length of the shots would only frighten them. That meant I had to produce a screenplay, and I went about that in an incredibly naive way. I took my joking remark about every sentence being like the description of a shot completely seriously. I divided the book up into so many scenes. I didn't cut anything out, but just took it as I found it. So I had a set number of scenes. I marked each one by lines in the text, and then broke them up into shots.

I didn't add anything either, and wrote a screenplay from the book; it has to be more faithful than any version of anything ever! Then Peter had to write in a couple of extra dialogues. There were places in the book where information was given in some other way, and where we needed to have dialogue. And there was one big change. The pre-history of the novel, what happens before it starts, namely that the hero is a goalkeeper and gets sent off on one occasion, I turned that into my opening sequence. Apart from that, it's closer to the book than any other film I've made.

*If you were so scrupulous about making your screenplay, did you stick to it while filming?*

I kept to it absolutely rigorously. I added the occasional shot, but without doing anything to the structure at all. I saw that film language sometimes demands a little more detail, and sometimes a little less than written language. But I never lost my sense of Peter's book as the description of the film I was trying to make.

*The film of yours that gives the strongest impression of following a screenplay is* The Scarlet Letter. *The pressures on that film are a lot stronger, as you're dealing with a historical theme. In historical films, the screenplay is a useful tool that helps the director organize the shoot, plan the costumes, the decor, the sets and so on.*

That's all true, but this film is about the worst example you could have of that. During the shooting of *The Scarlet Letter* I took many more liberties than I did with *The Goalkeeper's Fear of the Penalty.* I changed the text, the order of the scenes and the overall structure. I took some things out during the shoot, and I put in others. The point of departure was the screenplay that Tankred Dorst had written, but I made some changes to get us closer to Hawthorne's original novel. The whole thing was a pretty desperate undertaking anyway, because we originally wanted to shoot the film in the States, in New England, and ended up shooting it in Spain, on the coast of Galicia. The small parts were played not by American Puritans, but by Spanish Catholics, and our set was regularly used as a Wild West village. Our Indian was an ex-bullfighter with a gammy leg. These external conditions were such a handicap that I would change things just in the effort to hold the whole thing together in some way.

*How much did screenplays matter to you at the time anyway? What use did you make of them?*

Screenplays were pretty much news to me, I have to say. I'd made *Summer in the City* with a two- or three-page draft. The short films I made were entirely unscripted. There were just a couple of sketches of shots. I got into films via paintings, I was a painter. The notion of story was completely alien to me. It was a question of groping my way forward, and the screenplay had to be the most alien bit of film-making. The pressures from a screenplay were so new to me that I didn't even feel them as pressures at first, it was all just an adventure. I didn't start looking for a more relaxed relationship with screenplays until much later.

*When was that?*

On *False Movement.*

*So we're talking about 1974/5, a couple of years after* Alice in the Cities. *The story to* False Movement *was again something you and Peter Handke collaborated on.*

We'd had the idea of doing a version of *Wilhelm Meister's Apprenticeship* back when we were still making the *Goalie.* Peter wrote the screenplay all on his own, and it was almost 100 per cent dialogue. Hardly any instructions to camera or scene setting. The changes I made were entirely confined to the itinerary. I changed some of the places, but otherwise I followed the screenplay very closely. When I work with Peter – much more than with other writers I've worked with – I always take what he gives me very seriously.

*I find that quite remarkable, and suspect that it's for reasons not strictly to do with film. It's to do with your respect for the literary quality of his texts.*

Absolutely.

*And when his scripts are basically dialogue, like a play script, then of course that leaves you a lot of freedom as a director.*

That was always one of the great things about working with Peter, that he left me free to think about the shots and structure I wanted.

*So what is it makes you want to turn these texts into films? Was it that you were already agreed on subject-matter, or what gives you the impulse to find images for a text, to film a text?*

I think you have to begin by recognizing that what the characters say is a big part of a film. Here in Germany it's often been done in a fairly slapdash kind of way, or it's been shoved way down the pecking order. I've made several films that I scripted myself: *Alice in the Cities, Kings of the Road, The State of Things.* But I was never entirely happy with the results. Each time the dialogue seemed like a weakness to me. Sometimes it was all right; I think in *Alice* it's pretty much okay. But on *Kings of the Road* I remember sweating blood to get the characters even to open their mouths. So imagine what a relief it is to have a text in front of you like Peter's *False Movement.* A text can give you room, leave you free to work on other things. If you can put your trust in it, if what the characters say is good, then you have more energy for making the film, for working with the actors, for location work, and dealing with the crew. But it's important too that the script remain just a part of the film, and not claim to be the whole of it.

*It seems to me that so far as you're concerned, the characters' lines are the essential part of a screenplay. It contains other things besides, but those are all things you expect to be able to deal with during the shoot, or just improvise them.*

Yes. And the writing is especially important if there are several characters who have to be distinguished from each other. To tailor a part for a certain character is pretty demanding. Having different characters speaking in different ways, each of them 'in character', is a real art.

*You mean a sort of linguistic or acoustic signature that corresponds to their externals or their wardrobe.*

Yes, I think that's a real art. Even though, in the age of the writer-director, it's rather looked down on. But then I think those films often are let down because they don't display any particular skill in that department.

*But it's the rise of the writer-director that's contributed to the loss of that skill. It was driven out by the arrival of the* auteur *film.*

That's true; it's something I regret.

*Now if you, as a leading* auteur, *are prepared to say this, that surely heralds a change in attitude towards screenplay writing. The dialogue, as you said, is obviously the part of a screenplay that goes most directly into the completed film. But there are other important elements too, such as narrative position, rhythm and structure, that also have some bearing. But I don't think you see it that way.*

No, on that level, I wouldn't want to be dictated to by a screenplay, and I couldn't accept it either as a source of authority or a model. Nothing written can approximate to the feeling you get while you're making a film, the feeling for the style, the look, the idiom of a film. I think it's utterly mistaken if a screenplay prescribes those things too much, or even tries to prescribe them at all. Peter Handke always had a very clear understanding of that, which is why it was always good working with him, and why we managed to remain friends too.

*Because you each have your distinct creative areas. There's a clear separation, and that makes the relationship easier.*

Right. And Peter never supposed he'd written the whole film, and all that remained for me to do was shoot it. That's often how a writer and a director get into conflict. The writer 'sees' too much while writing, and is disappointed by what he actually sees afterwards.

*There's one film of yours that stands apart from the others, because it's your only genre work:* The American Friend. *It's a thriller, based on Patricia Highsmith's novel* Ripley's Game. *In genre films, the story plays a much bigger role than in an* auteur *film. There's a whole series of conventions to do with narrative, various rules that you need to be aware of. In* The American Friend *you deal with all that.*

Thrillers were always the books that meant the most to me. I could never get enough of Hammett or Chandler or Ross Macdonald. I would love to have been able to make a film with that kind of material. Among contemporary genre writers, Patricia Highsmith has all the right attributes. Her books have a psychological depth to them that's quite rare in genre writing, and she's very contemporary, she's writing about our time. In the novel that I filmed, there's an awful lot of plot and structure, to the extent that when I tried to tell someone the story, I would invariably get some of it wrong! That amount of plot and intrigue was difficult for me, and I wanted to make a bit of room for myself. So I inverted the geography. I had Ripley going from Germany to France to commit his murder, instead of from France to Germany. I'd thought, completely naively, that that wouldn't affect the story, but it ended up having quite serious consequences. And then when I cast Dennis Hopper as Ripley, that was like lobbing a hand grenade into the whole thing. I have to say I liked the effect of the hand grenade. It tore some huge holes, and we had to patch them up, and that took the film off in the direction of improvization and change.

*The directors who are your models – whom you idolize, whom you refer to in your films, like Ray and Lang – they all worked within those genre structures. Under the prevailing conditions, they always took their stories from books, and they worked from screenplays . . .*

I have to take issue with you there. According to Nick Ray, he had four or five pages of script when he started shooting *The Lusty Men*. Other films were improvised too during filming. Hawks gave his actors their lines on handwritten bits of paper every morning. And Fuller says there was the most incredible chaos a lot of the time in Hollywood, and hence a lot of room for change in the American productions of the period.

*All right, but even if things were written in short order, it was by writers, people working in the story departments of the studios. It may have been like an industrial process, but it was still done by writers, who kept a professional eye on the structures of their stories.*

I understand what you're saying. Times were different, and it was a different business. And the directors weren't their own producers either, the way I have been – except on *Hammett*.

*I'm sure* Hammett *wasn't a happy experience for you. But maybe it could illustrate the status of the screenplay in our time, in American productions of the 1980s. What part did the screenplay have in the four-year production history of that particular project?*

I think *Hammett* would be an example of the screenplay as finished article. The screenplay was expected to give an exact idea of the film that would then just have to be shot. All the ideas and the creativity that I generally brought to the shooting process were all expected of me in advance. I had never worked like that before.

*There were a whole host of writers working on the screenplay. I don't think all of them are even mentioned in the literature.*

All the names appear in the credits, regardless how big or small their contributions were.

*The Writers' Guild of America has very strict guidelines about credits, and it has a tribunal writers can go to, in case there's a disagreement.*

The first author on *Hammett* was Joe Gores, who wrote the novel the whole thing was based on. He was really too attached to the novel to be able to give us a proper script, and said so himself. So he bowed out of the project, quite amicably, and told us to get someone else. Then Tom Pope came along, with whom I went a long way towards describing the kind of film I wanted to make. The two of us completed a screenplay that I put all the sort of work into which with me usually goes into the actual filming. In a sense that was already the film. Francis Coppola thought that version was more like a film about a detective than a detective film. He wanted to play safe, so we turned our screenplay into a radio play, with all the dialogue, the sound effects, footfall, gunshots, music and everything. That was quite an amazing thing. We had Gene Hackman playing the other character, and Sam Shepard playing Hammett. But Coppola still wasn't convinced. So we took the idea of script as film one stage further, and I got together with a sketch artist, and we drew pictures for it. So we ran the radio play as a kind of ninety-minute soundtrack over our sketches and presented the whole thing as a video tape. But when we showed it to Coppola he didn't like it, and I don't really see how he could have done either, as a film that wasn't a film. So after a year and a half working on it, we got to the point where we had to start all over again.

*But didn't that version give you the feeling of being a very good approximation to your own idea of the film? Couldn't you have used it as a blueprint, and still had the creative tension and space to make the thing as a film?*

I'm not so sure. I went a very long way towards writing the film I wanted to make in advance. But that film didn't suit Cappola's ideas. It was too much of an *auteur* film – one author on another, at that. He wanted more action, so he and a writer called Dennis O'Flaherty sat down for a couple of weeks and did their own version. That script was the opposite of what we started off with, it was a pure action film. So I said, no, sorry, I can't do that, and this isn't what I want to make. Coppola agreed with me and told me to get together with Dennis O'Flaherty and take those elements from the second script that were missing from the first. A lot of the second went into the version that Dennis and I did, because visually and structurally it had a lot going for it. And that then became the version we started shooting. In the course of the shoot I changed a lot of things, because I hadn't worked on it the way I had on Pope's. I had doubts about things and rewrote them, or got Dennis to rewrite them. Then, a week before the end of the shoot, it became clear to me that the film I was shooting was going to need a different ending to the one in the script.

*And at that stage there was a break in the shoot, so you could get a new ending.*

I thought it was a wonderful luxury to be able to break off the shoot, and edit in peace, and write the ending. But the rough cut I showed Coppola was too slow, he thought. And by then he had the distributor on his back too, wanting more action. Dennis O'Flaherty was got rid of, and in his place they hired Ross Thomas, who had written a couple of good thrillers. He was to keep as much of the rough cut as possible, add some new detail, and provide the ending. He ended up rewriting one part, and adding a completely new female character, so in the end two-thirds of the film had to be reshot. I finished up on set only shooting what was there in front of me, just to get the thing finished.

*There are obviously a lot of special factors here, like the role of Coppola, but it does have certain typical aspects too: the script as object of speculation, and as a way of minimizing the risk, including the aesthetic risk. Now having seen the film, I readily believe the original version of the screenplay would probably have made the better film. So much chopping and changing must tend to make you lose sight of the real heart of the story and the material. After going through that experience, I expect you were only able to see a screenplay as a production 'instrument.'*

Yes, as an instrument of control. I was in a real hole at the time, as far as screenplays were concerned. I had started on another project for another studio, MGM. That was a film called *Trapdoor*, which I was going to shoot even before the final touches were put on *Hammett*. I'd taken the job and written a screenplay with Bill Kirby about computer crime. There was even a cast in place, but three or four weeks before we were due to begin shooting, it was suddenly shelved without any reason being given. That happens quite regularly in the States. Of 1,000 screenplays, only 100 ever land on a producer's desk; of those 100, ten go into production, and of those ten only one is actually made. So after my experience with *Trapdoor*, I'd really had it with screenplays.

*That feeling is very clearly expressed in the film you made during the four-year wrangling over* Hammett. *In* The State of Things, *your alter ego, the German director Friedrich talks pretty disparagingly about scripts, as though they were what drove the life out of a film. He says stories have too many rules and a film with a story is dead, it leaves no room for life. You're pretty vitriolic on the topic in* The State of Things. *Is that still your position today?*

No, that was based on my circumstances at the time, it was a pretty extreme and one-sided position – and I knew it.

*At the end, there's this wonderful scene where your director Friedrich and the producer who's running away from his creditors, are driving through Los Angeles at night in a caravan, just as it's getting light. You have Gordon saying a film without a story is like a house without walls. Friedrich disagrees, he says he'd rather build his films on the spaces between the characters.*

I took that rather extreme position on purpose, and took it as far as it would go into the film – *ad absurdum* really. The little bit of story and screenplay in that largely improvised film occurs at the end, in that meeting between producer and director, and the death of both of them. That unexpected bit of fiction saved the film. Without it, the film would have just collapsed in a heap. And so in the end, the film disproves its own thesis about stories.

*That sounds as though you've come to accept the need for stories and the structure that having a screenplay affords.*

I have trouble with the walls in my films, that's true enough. But, as I say, Friedrich gets proved wrong. That scrap of fiction helped the film 'no end', more than I would have thought possible. In order to imagine the spaces and define them, you need walls. After *The State of Things*, I thought: now or never. Either you put that thesis to rest by showing what you've learned from this film, or you haven't really got a future in this business. That's why I tried to make *Paris, Texas* quite stringently after a story.

*But surely that's a film that really doesn't have much of a structure. Sam Shepard's book* Motel Chronicles *– on which it's based – is a loose collection of short prose pieces. It's more atmosphere than narrative. And I didn't think Shepard wrote the screenplay either, I thought it was Kid Carson.*

No, no. Sam and I wrote the screenplay together, all Kid Carson did was help on the structure of the second half, by which time Sam was no longer involved. But we wrote the story together to the point where the father and son leave LA together. Up to that point, all the scenes and dialogues were written out.

*I'm amazed. That really isn't my sense of the film at all. When I saw it the second time,* Paris, Texas *had lost a lot of its intensity for me. The structuring moment that retrieves* The State of Things *and gives it an ending, just isn't there in* Paris, Texas. *The film seems to spread out more and more towards the end, but without ever really finding itself either. Early on, it has the intensity and the atmosphere of its different components, the camerawork and the short scenes and the music; the emotional intensity of its detail. But as a story it just doesn't come together. And when you see it the second time, you see that very clearly; everything falls to pieces, crumbles away. The film seems completely improvised and two-dimensional.*

There may be something in that. The second part of *Paris, Texas* we were flying blind. And because the first part was so tightly structured, I supposed it shows. Even so, there's this momentum that takes you all the way through to the end – even if the film then loses some of its shape and intensity, especially in the long scene between Travis and his wife at the peepshow.

*But that momentum you talk about is purely external, if not superficial. The State of Things does have a kind of inner coherence that keeps the most unlikely bits together, a kind of skeleton. In* Paris, Texas *there's only the scaffolding of driving, of the road.*

Yes, but that's an American tradition and Sam Shepard, the writer, is responsible for that.

*In your newest film,* Wings of Desire, *you seem to have come full circle. It's a film with a literary model, that's part improvised, and that was again made with the collaboration of Peter Handke.*

Yes, the film had a fragmentary screenplay, merely my attempts to structure the whole thing. But there were also ten texts that Peter Handke gave us, which we worked on together very early on in the project. I told Peter my very rudimentary idea of the story. It was a story that could spin out of control any time, because the angels, my subject, could get into any imaginable situation. The problem with the story wasn't so much making things up for it, but keeping some control of one's imagination. Peter had just finished *The Repetition*, and felt drained. After a week of going for walks together, he said: I understand this and that bit of your film, I can imagine writing some lines or maybe something more like a poem. He didn't want to write a screenplay, more like a theatre piece. The ten passages he ended up writing were like islands in the vast ocean of possible ideas I had for the film. And as we shot it, we had to keep making sure we reached the next island, get a bit of solid ground under our feet, and then row on in the dark. I got a lot of help, especially ideas for scenes, from Richard Reitinger. But Peter's texts were the pillars that carried the whole film.

*I remember you had to write some kind of screenplay to show to backers and subsidy committees. Was that job, having to present something in writing, just a chore, or did it bring you any nearer to your conception of the film?*

Of course it was a step nearer. It wasn't just a chore, it also meant I was moving closer to the film. The attempt to write something down to show juries or producers or backers is also an honest attempt on my part to grasp the film. Those texts that are written to persuade institutions that you know what you're doing are useful, even if they set things out in a form in which I don't actually need them to be. On my next film I'm going to be working from a complete screenplay. For the first time since *The American Friend* I'll be filming *To the End of the World* from a full script. And I can tell you I'm quite happy about that.

*First appeared in*: Writing for the Screen. Screenplay as Alternative Mode of Narration, *ed. Jochen Brunow, edition text + kritik, Munich,*
*1988*